INSANITY in the CHURCH

The Powerful Delusion Sent by God

INSANITY in the CHURCH

The Powerful Delusion Sent by God

Timothy Williams

WINEPRESS WP PUBLISHING

Printed in the United States of America.

Cover design: His Workmanship

Packaged by WinePress Publishing,
PO Box 428, Enumclaw, WA 98022.

Unless otherwise noted, all Scriptures are taken from the Holy Bible, New International Version, Copyright © 1973, 1978, 1984 by the International Bible Society. Used by permission of Zondervan Publishing House. The "NIV" and "New International Version" trademarks are registered in the United States Patent and Trademark Office by International Bible Society.

Scripture references marked KJV are taken from the King James Version of the Bible.

ISBN 1-57921-390-1
Library of Congress Catalog Card Number: 2001090522

THANKS

Special thanks to my wife, Carla, who stands steadfast beside me giving God time to crucify me.

A wife of noble character is her husband's crown . . .
(Proverbs 12:4)

Dedicated to those who love God more than the pleasure of the Powerful Delusion.

For this reason God sends them a powerful delusion. (2 Thessalonians 2:11)

CONTENTS

FOREWORD

"Reveille!" The sound of reveille was the last thing most of us wanted to hear so early in the morning. Another day of boot camp, another day of field training. Webster's Dictionary defines the meaning of reveille: "to wake up" or "to watch." In the times we live in, the church desperately needs a wake up call—a trumpet sound that rouses her from her complacency. The church has ignored or silenced the few honest watchmen who strive to bring her to repentance. *Insanity in the Church: The Powerful Delusion Sent by God* gives a clear "Reveille" call and warning to the church.

Jesus taught in Matthew 7:13–14 that the road to salvation is narrow and few will find it; "Enter through the narrow gate. For wide is the gate and broad is the road that leads to destruction, and many enter through it. But small is the gate and narrow the road that leads to life, and only a few find it." After twelve years in the "wide road," "cheap grace" church, I finally heard God say that the full message that leads to life was not preached. Tim Williams reveals the reason the church today has taken the wrong road.

Like a ship off course, the church has missed God's chosen path—the way of the cross. We have lost the determination of the apostle Paul when he said, "For I resolved to know nothing while I was with you except Jesus Christ and him crucified," (1 Corinthians 2:2). A ship off course, even a fraction, over time and distance will miss its intended destination by hundreds, even thousands of miles. So the church has gotten off the course that leads to picking up its cross. She no longer makes disciples of all men, as Jesus commanded, but instead makes worldly, carnal Christians, who know nothing of denying self and suffering in their bodies to be done with sin, (1 Peter 4:1).

The leaders in the church today preach what the people want to hear, each generation straying further off course. We have been carried from one false teaching to another during the past hundred years, as Ephesians 4:14 states; "tossed back and forth by the waves, and blown here and there by every wind of teaching and by the cunning and craftiness of men in their deceitful scheming." *Insanity in the Church*, speaks the truth in love about the false humility and teachings prevalent today, in the hope that we may "in all things grow up into him who is the Head, that is, Christ," (Ephesians 4:15).

The belt of Truth (Ephesians 6:14) has been stripped from the church. Tim Williams reveals the foundational truths we have removed or twisted. I challenge you not to dismiss any of these things, thinking they do not apply to you. Search your heart and see what false teachings have enticed you to take the easy wide road. A time is coming when it will be impossible to hear the reveille. God will send a powerful delusion so that the church will believe the lies they have so long embraced, (2 Thessalonians 2:11) The biblical truths spoken in this book must return to the pulpits if we have any hope of standing against this powerful delusion coming in the last days. It's time to listen to this wake up call that demands that we return to God's intended course of holiness.

Dennis Myers

Chapter 1

THE LIE

Heinrich Himmler, the organizer of Hitler's SS Army and overseer of the extermination of millions of Jews, studied agriculture before the war. He wanted to be a farmer. If Himmler had never joined Hitler, the world would never know the monstrous heart he possessed. Hitler himself dreamed of becoming an artist, but the conditions in Germany provided fertile ground to work the seeds of destruction. The same is true for us. The opportunity to sin may not yet present itself, but that does not mean we too do not have a monster hidden inside our hearts.

A time fast approaches when the door will open for the wickedness in each man to come to life, if he has not died to self. The opportunity comes in the form of a lie invading the church and sweeping the world today. This lie penetrates every aspect of the church and the right circumstance will allow the monster to arise. This hidden lie, deceiving the Christian world, is the Powerful Delusion that Paul warns us about.

> For this reason God sends them a powerful delusion so that they will believe the lie and so that all will be condemned who have not believed the truth but have delighted in wickedness. (2 Thessalonians 2:11)

This book does not focus on the errors of a specific revival movement, church, denomination, ministry, or person for two reasons. First, none of us can stand before God innocent and declare we are untouched by the delusion. Secondly, Scripture should motivate us to repent without the need to point out the faults of another. It is far too easy to build a church or ministry, or to sell a book by pointing out the faults of another. There are always objectors to any group or person. Using lurid gossip to get individuals to side on an issue does not kill the monster in our own hearts. In other words, it is easy to look at others and think we are not like them. That is why Jesus bids us to look at our own lives, rather than someone else's. The words of Jesus telling us "no" carry even more weight as we approach the last days. For "unless" we "repent" we will also "perish."

> Or those eighteen who died when the tower in Siloam fell on them—do you think they were more guilty than all the others living in Jerusalem? I tell you, no! But unless you repent, you too will all perish. (Luke 13:4–5)

God Sends the Delusion

Unless we repent by hating our own life[1] and suffering with Christ, which we will talk more about later, God will make sure we believe the lie. Right now God, not Satan, sends the "Powerful Delusion." Look again at 2 Thessalonians 2:11; "For this reason *God* sends them a powerful delusion so that they will believe the lie."

God allows and permits rather than hinders the work of Satan so that circumstances arise that expose each man's heart. Like Himmler, who only needed a Hitler, God will bring about a situation that reveals the wickedness in our hearts. There will be no gray areas and no doubts about where a man stands. There will be no lying words that cover up man's heart. Each man will be shown for who he really is. Whether religious or atheist, the heat will be turned up so that the evil in a man will rise to the surface for all to

14

see. If you have been fooling yourself about your relationship with Jesus, you will find out the truth.

A "Powerful Delusion" is a powerful lie. It is faith, strong faith in something false. Right now, as you read these words God is causing a strong faith in a false Jesus to take place. In this book we will look at the true Jesus in order to expose the lie. Genuine faith can only happen by loving the Truth. And a love for the Truth can only happen as we die to self. It is the message of the offensive cross that crucifies self so we might have a sincere love for the Truth.

The Lawless One

The delusion or lie comes with great power and authority. Believing in the false Jesus is easy. Outward circumstances make it seem as if the lie stands on a firm foundation. Yet, in reality its foundation is the "lawless one" spoken about in 2 Thessalonians. Hitler's regime looked like it had a strong foundation, but it crumbled when the truth was revealed. The Hitler for our hearts will be the "lawless one." Just like Hitler promised freedom and prosperity, a form of Christianity based upon a false freedom will allow man to abandon the restraints of holy worship. The false Jesus will come with "all kinds of counterfeit miracles, signs and wonders." There will literally be "all kinds" of manifestations, feelings, and confirmations preparing the way for the "lawless one." Right now on any given Sunday, preacher after preacher talks about new freedom in Christ. But such freedom is a lie and has nothing to do with the true and holy Jesus.

> The coming of the lawless one will be in accordance with the work of Satan displayed in all kinds of counterfeit miracles, signs and wonders, and in every sort of evil that deceives those who are perishing. They perish because they refused to love the truth and so be saved. (2 Thessalonians 2:9–10)

"They perish because they refused to love the truth," is the explanation God gives for allowing the Powerful Delusion to work within the church. Instead of loving the Truth, they at best only give lip service to it—they are mockers. The Powerful Delusion comes with "every sort of evil." From those who love the emotional worship to those who embrace a calmer style, the lie still works its magic. Even among those who talk of the cross, the offense is missing.

Unity

This lie sweeps the world today. It is a lie that both Christians and non-Christians believe without realizing it. This falsehood brings all men together in unity. All half-truths and full-blown heresies, all subtle compromises in the church converge together under a single banner. But the change is so slow and gradual that few honestly realize what is happening. Yet, the entire world will unite when the anti-Christ comes on the scene. Men will look at each other in amazement, suddenly realizing they have been believing and preaching in agreement with one another for a long time. In ever so subtle ways, the same message is embraced throughout the world and in the worldly church. Whether atheist or Christian, there is unity under one lie chanted by all. Pulpits by the thousands preach it while the world promotes it. Even those at odds with each other are taken in by the same single lie.

For the first time in the history of the world a great confirmation of a lie on a global scale is occurring. When the evidence is weighed and the facts established, the world and the church will conclude and agree that this lie is really truth. If it were not for the grace of God in the small remnant of the elect, everyone would believe the lie. A gift of healing will manifest in a powerful way, and the whole world will be "astonished." So astonished, that everyone in the world, except for the elect, will be persuaded to follow the beast.

> One of the heads of the beast seemed to have had a fatal wound, but the fatal wound had been healed. The whole world was astonished and followed the beast. (Revelation 13:3)

God allows confirmation of the lie through miracles, signs, and wonders. For even as the Mormons have a burning in the bosom to affirm their lie, and others speak in tongues to confirm their "truth," so too God validates the lie in Christian churches world-wide.

The Original Lie Continues

Please understand that God still works true miracles, but we live in a time period when we need the utmost discernment.[2] This lie or Powerful Delusion, is not a new lie, but the same ancient ruse told to Adam and Eve in the Garden of Eden. The delusion tells people that they can be "as God," taking matters in their own hands, living their own life, applying Scripture as they see fit, and still live forever. The deception that we "will not die" as man seeks to bless himself with Scripture, is the same lie of the Powerful Delusion told in the Garden.

> but God did say, 'You must not eat fruit from the tree that is in the middle of the garden, and you must not touch it, or you will die.'" "You will not surely die," the serpent said to the woman. "For God knows that when you eat of it your eyes will be opened, and you will be like God, knowing good and evil." (Genesis 3:3–5)

Satan deceived man once, and the same lie that sweeps the world, will end with the anti-Christ declaring himself to be God. The lie told to man in the Garden of Eden, that we can be "like God," will come to its fullest level by the anti-Christ and Satan. The whole world will finally achieve perfect good self-esteem. The good self-esteem we give ourselves because of what we have created. It would not surprise me if the anti-Christ turns out to be a cloned man, the "work of our hands" for which Satan gives the power to do amazing, miraculous things. The lie is then confirmed that we can create a perfect man with god-like, God-given talents. But as the following Scripture declares, to worship the "work of" our "hands" is to worship "demons."

The rest of mankind that were not killed by these plagues still did not repent of the work of their hands; they did not stop worshiping demons, and idols of gold, silver, bronze, stone and wood—idols that cannot see or hear or walk. (Revelation 9:20)

Satan deceived man from the beginning that he would not suffer or die. Man continues today to believe the lie that he can be successful without the cross crucifying self. Religious man believes that he can command God if he has enough faith. The Powerful Delusion tells the church that we can use all the power of self to win numbers to Christ and not be sinful in God's sight. In all of its various manifestations, we can reduce the lie in the church to one statement.

Man is acceptable to God without crucifixion of self by the power of His Holy Spirit.

Like Adam and Eve, many Christians today believe we can strive to be "as god" and become godly without suffering or dying on the cross to overcome sin.[3] We think God wants to bless our plans and dreams, without utter death to self. But only those who "share" in the "sufferings of Christ" go to heaven. We become "co-heirs with Christ, if *indeed* we share in his sufferings."

Now if we are children, then we are heirs—heirs of God and co-heirs with Christ, if indeed we share in his sufferings in order that we may also share in his glory. (Romans 8:17)

Refuse to Love the Truth

The Christian Church possesses the greatest risk in being duped by the delusion. A gospel close to the truth, without actually being true, is the most deadly. We need not fear the atheist for we know where he stands. Yet the one who reads Scripture from a spirit of self becomes our most dangerous enemy. Indeed, our greatest enemy is ourselves as we read and love the Scriptures, but reject the work of the cross.[4] It is great darkness to speak of holiness, righteousness, carrying our crosses, and glorifying God, when loving self is the motivation. God is strengthening this lie in millions today who lay hold of His name. Millions upon millions of people believe the delusion in spite of strong evidence of its falsehood. Many fall prey to this slow "deluding," and subtle indulgence of self and sin, even as they quote Scripture. They enlarge their influence, territory, and blessings in the name of the Lord, but it is the glorification of themselves they really seek.

Christians everywhere refuse to accept the evidence against the lie because they love themselves more than God. When conviction comes from the Holy Spirit, they say, "there is no condemnation in Christ." When a preacher speaks of obeying God's commands by the Holy Spirit, they call it legalism. When the Holy Spirit points out ways in which they serve Jesus only for what they can get from Him, they reject it as too hard a gospel. As Scripture declares, "They perish because they refuse to love the truth." They do not love all of Scripture, only the ones that feed their flesh and make them feel good. They do not love true righteousness, but idolize the blessings they receive.

Forsaken by God?

Since they refuse to let go of the vilest form of idolatry, the worship of self, God works a poetic justice. He permits false Christianity to be confirmed as truth, while allowing true Christianity to be seen as a lie. The closing of time for wickedness on earth will find men fully rejecting the cross of Christ. We do well to remember that men crucified Jesus when the tree was green.[5] Now that the tree is dry and the fullness of the message of the cross draws to an end, we see a reflection of our time period in Jesus' death. For when Jesus stood on the very pinnacle of victory, His life, His teachings, His words all appeared false. The same remains true for all who understand and truly walk the crucified life. The false church has so much power it is easy to think something must be wrong with the true message of the cross. Like Jesus who, at the peak of His weakness, wondered where God was, true Christians in the last days will cry the same thing.

And at the ninth hour Jesus cried out in a loud voice, "Eloi, Eloi, lama sabachthani?"—which means, "My God, my God, why have you forsaken me?" (Mark 15:34)

True Christians wonder why God leaves them so powerless when the false and empty teaching in Christ's name remains so powerful. Like the Pharisees and the mob that gathered around Jesus to watch Him die, those who love self gather around to taunt those who are being crucified with Christ. The temptation to come down off the cross is very great because false Christianity appears blessed and successful. The weakness of true Christians, however, will condemn false ones someday, and in God's timing, they will be resurrected. False teachers may promote themselves and their ministries while others become weaker and weaker. But if you pick up your cross, be of good courage, the resurrected life of Christ will soon be yours in His fullness and glory. Just don't become afflicted yourself with the madness infecting the worldly church. Man is insanely in love with himself even as he talks about denying self, and God lets this mental illness grow.

Those suffering from spiritual mental illness delude and deceive themselves and others, about what constitutes sound judgment. They are unable to discern reality from dreams, lies from truth. To an insane man, whatever he believes becomes his truth. The seeds of which can be seen in comments like, "Whatever you believe is fine;" or "That's just your interpretation." To discern the vileness of the insanity in the church one must step back for a moment and ponder what is happening.

As this lie grows, the falsehood in the church also increases. It is God's way of disciplining the church for its lukewarmness and hostility toward the Truth. God will work perfect justice by paying back those who have not fully embraced the Truth—picking up the cross of Christ in their lives. They may speak of the cross, but they have no longing for that cross to be applied to their lives.

Bad News

The message of the cross spells bad news for our flesh. It is a negative gospel to our sinful nature and to those who believe the lie. They hate the message of the cross and seek desperately to alter its meaning. Those drawn into the Powerful Delusion fully reject and fight against this message because it bears bad news. Like the king of Israel and Jehoshaphat, the king of Judah, they want to hear good news from the prophets, even if it's false.

> Dressed in their royal robes, the king of Israel and Jehoshaphat king of Judah were sitting on their thrones at the threshing floor by the entrance to the gate of Samaria, with all the prophets prophesying before them. Now Zedekiah son of Kenaanah had made iron horns, and he declared, "This is what the Lord says: 'With these you will gore the Arameans until they are destroyed.'" All the other prophets were prophesying the same thing. "Attack Ramoth Gilead and be victorious," they said, "for the Lord will give it into the king's hand." (2 Chronicles 18:9–11)

Jehoshaphat and the king of Israel enjoyed hearing from the false prophets who promised victory and prosperity not promised by God. But let a true prophet speak, and they try to persuade him to lie.

> The messenger who had gone to summon Micaiah said to him, "Look, as one man the other prophets are predicting success for the king. Let your word agree with theirs, and speak favorably." But Micaiah said, "As surely as the Lord lives, I can tell him only what my God says." (2 Chronicles 18:12–13)

Jehoshaphat and the king of Israel hated the true prophet, Micaiah, because he "never prophesies anything good." The prophets before him prophesied lies and they loved it. Micaiah, however, prophesied death and disaster. The truth of the message of the cross tells us that we must destroy the self that lives in us. At its core is a message of death and there is no resurrected life without death to self. This thoroughly frustrates most "Christians." Many find the message of the cross negative, legalistic, and unloving because they do not want to lose their lives for Jesus.[6] Instead, they worship Jesus in the fullness of the sinful flesh and to such individuals God sends a "lying spirit."

More than likely right now someone works this spiritual lie in your church. Indeed, you may be the one that God uses to move the Powerful Delusion forward. You could be the "spiritual person" with wisdom, insight, or even dreams from God in order to lie to the people. The Powerful Delusion is an "enticing" message confirmed by "all" of the "prophets." With every passing day, more and more individuals demonstrate that the Powerful Delusion is true. They feel in their spirits that it is true. God has proven to them that the lie is the truth. The Powerful Delusion is divine justice, a paying back in a way we deserve to be paid back. For if we claim to carry our cross for Jesus, but live a lie, God will repay us with a lie for the lie we lived. Only He knows how many millions will find the Powerful Delusion to be a "disaster." Just as Micaiah told Jehoshaphat, God permits a "lying spirit" to sweep the church.

> The king of Israel said to Jehoshaphat, "Didn't I tell you that he never prophesies anything good about me, but only bad?" Micaiah continued, "Therefore hear the word of the Lord: I saw the Lord sitting on his throne with all the host of heaven standing on his right and on his left. And the Lord said, 'Who will entice Ahab king of Israel into attacking Ramoth Gilead and going to his death there?' "One suggested this, and another that. Finally, a spirit came forward, stood before the Lord and said, 'I will entice him.' "'By what means?' the Lord asked. "'I will go and be a lying spirit in the mouths of all his prophets,' he said. "'You will succeed in enticing him,' said the Lord. 'Go and do it.' "So now the Lord has put a lying spirit in the mouths of these prophets of yours. The Lord has decreed disaster for you." (2 Chronicles 18:17–22)

We love a lie, so God gives us what we want. We refuse to surrender unto death to be able to love the truth, so God agrees to a spirit's suggestion to be a "lying spirit" in the "mouths of all his prophets." So should it really surprise us that within churches today all the prophets, teachers, and leaders prophesy the same lie? We live in the last days when Jesus declared that most people's love for God would grow cold. Most who profess Christianity are actually cold in their love for God and constantly compromise the truth. Sure, they cling to certain doctrines that show others wrong, but there is a vast difference between pointing out error and loving the Truth. Since vast numbers of individuals follow Jesus for what they can get from Him, rather than picking up a cross and dying to self, God sends a delusion so they will believe a lie. The delusion overcomes anyone who will not hate his or her own life. Anyone who does not discover how to hate his life, by the power of the Holy Spirit, does not have "eternal life."

> The man who loves his life will lose it, while the man who hates his life in this world will keep it for eternal life. (John 12:25)

False Gospel

The Powerful Delusion, the church forsaking the message of the cross, is part of God's plan to usher in the anti-Christ. Those who love Jesus need to rebuke and remove themselves from churches and individuals refusing to deny self. Those who love the Lord must prepare themselves to be run over by the false church. As Daniel 12:7 declares, once the "power of the holy people has been finally broken" the anti-Christ will arise. As the false church increases in power, true Christians will become powerless. The world and the worldly in the church will come together in unity. God will allow the lying spirit to replace the message of the cross with the Powerful Delusion—a false gospel, that comes with many miracles and much fanfare.

> The man clothed in linen, who was above the waters of the river, lifted his right hand and his left hand toward heaven, and I heard him swear by him who lives forever, saying, "It will be for a time, times and half a time. When the power of

the holy people has been finally broken, all these things will be completed." I heard, but I did not understand. So I asked, "My lord, what will the outcome of all this be?" He replied, "Go your way, Daniel, because the words are closed up and sealed until the time of the end. Many will be purified, made spotless and refined, but the wicked will continue to be wicked. None of the wicked will understand, but those who are wise will understand. (Daniel 12:7–10)

The Powerful Delusion will refine and purify those who truly love God. But they will have to be wise and understanding. The time period fast approaching gives the anti-Christ power through his "flattery" and persuasive words. Flattery is the calling card of the Powerful Delusion. We love flattery, and that gives the false message its power. The Powerful Delusion will cause many who love the Lord to stumble in their walk because they fall prey to flattery.

"His armed forces will rise up to desecrate the temple fortress and will abolish the daily sacrifice. Then they will set up the abomination that causes desolation. With flattery he will corrupt those who have violated the covenant, but the people who know their God will firmly resist him. "Those who are wise will instruct many, though for a time they will fall by the sword or be burned or captured or plundered. When they fall, they will receive a little help, and many who are not sincere will join them. Some of the wise will stumble, so that they may be refined, purified and made spotless until the time of the end, for it will still come at the appointed time. (Daniel 11:31–35)

God told Daniel that many who are "not sincere" will join the church. As this happens, even the best churches weaken. The dynamic way the delusion arrives will cause some of the "wise" to stumble into accepting erroneous doctrines, attitudes, and false spirituality. In order to be "refined" the elect must repent of this sin and compromise. If you don't want to stumble when the anti-Christ comes on the scene, repent now of the "small" sins in your life that will blossom during the fullness of the Powerful Delusion. Right now Satan corrupts the church with "flattery" and we overlook "little sins" because we are blinded and dazzled by the attention and flattery Satan sends our way.

True Christians must "firmly resist" the Powerful Delusion now if they hope to resist the anti-Christ later. He will gain his power because the Powerful Delusion will break the strength of the church and allow the anti-Christ free reign. Therefore when the book of Revelation discusses the condition of the church during the reign of the anti-Christ, we must take it as a warning to tune out the overcoming "feel good" type of preachers. Let us have ears to hear what the Spirit says so we might remain strong and ready.

Options in the Last Days

The overcoming church will have one of three options in the last days. Let me repeat, there are only three options: enter captivity, be burned, or killed by the sword. As Daniel 11:34 stated, the wise will "fall by the sword," be "burned," or "captured." Daniel declares that the church will only receive a "little help" during the most distressing time the world has ever experienced. The church will not be victorious as the false teachers declare today. We will not be raptured out but will survive through "endurance and faithfulness." People who fall for the Powerful Delusion will not be prepared for this time period, to say the least. Daniel's list matches the following options given in Revelation.

> He who has an ear, let him hear. If anyone is to go into captivity, into captivity he will go. If anyone is to be killed with the sword, with the sword he will be killed. This calls for patient endurance and faithfulness on the part of the saints. (Revelation 13:9–10)

Garden Beginnings

Whatever you believe about the rapture, keep in mind the core of the Powerful Delusion is the worship of self and the pleasing of man. After all, the anti-Christ will be a man who perfectly worships himself. What started in the Garden of Eden, the temptation to become "like God," ends with a man declaring himself "to be God." Inside each of us hides the seed of thinking we can become as God and unless it has been crucified unto death, we will follow the anti-Christ. He will speak of being God and it will sound correct and true, if we have not died to self. At this point, both the atheist and the false believer in Jesus will discover they believe the same thing.

> He will oppose and will exalt himself over everything that is called God or is worshiped, so that he sets himself up in God's temple, proclaiming himself to be God. (2 Thessalonians 2:4)

The false Christian church will hear the talk of the anti-Christ and realize it has preached the same thing for years. Both proclaim a message of good self-esteem, finding one's life, and gaining the power God intended for man. However, that power was lost when we fell in the garden and will not return to man until he has fallen to the ground and died. We deceive ourselves when we believe that if the goal is noble our hearts must be right. No heart is totally pure until it has been crucified with Christ. No cause, even those for the kingdom of God, will result in good if we are not actively dead to self. Paul warned Timothy to "have nothing to do" with these false Christians and churches because they are lovers of self while claiming to know God.

> treacherous, rash, conceited, lovers of pleasure rather than lovers of God—having a form of godliness but denying its power. Have nothing to do with them. (2 Timothy 3:4–5)

How much closer to the last days we must be than in Timothy and Paul's time. The Powerful Delusion happens everywhere in every church. The root of loving self remains while the false Christians boast of their relationship with God. They brag with all the insanity they can muster of their works and experiences in God. Yet, all the talk of love is not really love, but self-righteous man doing good deeds in order to feel better about himself. True love only flows through those who hate their own lives, but such an offensive cross is just not present in the church.

Look closely again at the passage in 2 Timothy and see how it plays out in our churches today. Look at the rebellious children in the church today dressing and acting like the world. The "love for pleasure" is obvious in the picnics, parties, tanning, playing, cruises, fine dining, and having fun in the name of the Lord. Any church that teaches self-control by the Holy Spirit is mocked as legalistic and unloving. False Christians act "brutal" toward those who preach the message of the cross, yet quickly act on any impulse and claim to hear the voice of the Lord. Certainly, a gospel that works out one's salvation with fear and trembling is hotly rejected. If you begin to live and preach the message of the cross you will find out just how "brutal" these individuals and churches act.

The true church will know the power found in a crucified life, of losing one's life, and daily surrendering self. True Christians will have died to self so much every day, that when the time comes to fully give up their lives, God will grant them the grace they need. We will not look for comfort while picking up our crosses, but rejoice in the suffering.

Where can death to self be found in men leading seminars on carrying one's cross while promoting the golf courses, fine food, and fun in their brochures? How can they think they will overcome the anti-Christ with ease? Thinking we can claim the blood of Jesus, the promises of His Word, and still go to heaven, while we embrace the insanity of the world, is a Powerful Delusion indeed.

> They overcame him by the blood of the Lamb and by the word of their testimony; they did not love their lives so much as to shrink from death. (Revelation 12:11)

Anyone not hating his life in Truth and Spirit on a daily basis will never find the power to lay down his life when the anti-Christ makes his demands. Indeed, God will make sure that you take the mark of the beast. For it is not really Satan we fight against, but God who allows Satan to work in those who refuse to love the Truth.

> For this reason *God sends* them a powerful delusion so that they
> will believe the lie. (2 Thessalonians 2:11 emphasis added)

Note with fear and trembling that "God sends" the Powerful Delusion. In the last days, many ministers and teachers of the Word will step up first to take the mark of the beast. Many right now who speak a lot about the anti-Christ and the last days will surprise you on that day. God will send the "Powerful Delusion" into their hearts and they will gladly take the mark of the beast. For it is not the knowledge of the last days that saves a man, but whether on a daily basis he hated his own life and died to self. We fight not against Satan, but against God who is against all who reject the message of the cross. It is time for us to "kiss the Son" and cry out with all our hearts to understand and live the crucified life before the day of "wrath."

> Kiss the Son, lest he be angry and you be destroyed in your way,
> for his wrath can flare up in a moment. Blessed are all who take
> refuge in him. (Psalms 2:12)

Worship of Self

Again, what is the Powerful Delusion? Like a madman, it is believing something in spite of strong evidence to the contrary. For a false Christian, it is believing that we can be saved apart from the true cross of Christ in our lives. It is always amazing to watch someone when the blinders fall from their eyes. I know a man who shook his head in amazement after hearing this message and started to pick up the cross God had for him. He asked in wonderment, "Where was I at? I read all those scriptures before and even taught others about them. I heard emotion-packed sermons and read many books, but I never saw this before. Now I see it in every scripture, and can feel the effects of the cross in all that God does in my life."

The grandest delusion in the church today is that man can love his own life and still go to heaven. Satan loves to worship himself and perpetrates this lie in the name of Jesus. He uses Scripture, as evidenced by miracles, signs, and wonders to get us to bless self. While such miracles and evidence began slowly, they gain intensity with each passing year, to the point that it effects nearly every church. For a church to declare itself clean of this insanity, much effort will be needed to first cleanse the church and then to keep it clean. The Powerful Delusion and false revival will be so powerful that even the elect will take a second look and question their Christianity.

The cross must be measured against all works, worship, lives, and doctrines if the elect hope to find the grace to overcome. If you are indeed one of the elect, the Holy Spirit must immediately make real to you the following passage, for it will take great "resolve[d]" not to move from the true gospel.

> For I resolved to know nothing while I was with you except Jesus Christ and him crucified. (1 Corinthians 2:2)

If you have the power of the cross in your life, all of this will become clear to you. You will clearly see the false church and re-vival. You will not see it just because the logic of a book or sermon shows some faults in the false church, but because the cross gives you the power to see it. Let me repeat it again. Just because you have knowledge of the wickedness of the false church, doesn't mean you will not take the mark of the beast. God does not save a man because he has knowledge of the last days, but because daily, by grace he picks up his cross and follows Jesus.

> Then he said to them all: "If anyone would come after me, he must deny himself and take up his cross daily and follow me. For whoever wants to save his life will lose it, but whoever loses his life for me will save it." (Luke 9:23–24)

Only those who lose their lives will possess the power and grace not to be taken in by the Powerful Delusion. All those who have found their lives in their ministry, church, prayers, works, miracles, and bible studies will follow the anti-Christ, persecute true Chris-tians, and be judged apart from the blood of Jesus. All who enjoy their life in Christ, without a carrying cross of suffering unto death, live a lie and God will make sure they believe the Powerful Delusion. God will send whatever it takes to get them to believe. The spiritual feelings, answered prayers, miracles, numbers, insight into Scripture, open doors, healings, blessings, and more confirm the lie to all who will not hate their own lives.

Chapter 2

INSANITY

Are they servants of Christ? (I am out of my mind to talk like this.) I am more. I have worked much harder, been in prison more frequently, been flogged more severely, and been exposed to death again and again. (2 Corinthians 11:23)

I am . . .

Rev. Pastor Proud Heart
Prophet
Apostle
Spirit filled
Dr. Worldly
an in demand speaker
a dynamic leader
a pastor's pastor
Bishop
Deacon
Revivalist
Psalmist
a Bible thumper
a miracle worker
nationally and internationally known

the very reverend false humility
a powerful declarer of God's Word
anointed to bless you
a lover of God
a marriage counselor
able to slay others in the Spirit
able to cast out demons
recommended by big wigs in the church
a winner of the Dove Awards

I have . . .

taken a stand for the truth
baptized thousands
visited the Holy Land
studied the Greek and Hebrew
been binding and loosing for years
dreams and visions from God
the gift of tongues
a Ph. D. and other initials after my name
authored many books
been serving the Lord for over 20 years
won numerous writing awards.

My church has . . .

1,000's in attendance
awe inspiring worship
a new sanctuary
God's blessings
changed thousands of lives
the Holy Ghost moving through us
a cult-busting group
Four square gospel calls
a lively choir as featured in a major magazine
positive, relevant Bible teaching
a passion for Jesus

lasting friendships
impartation of revival fire
a friendly congregation interested in sharing God's love
great food and fun

Our ministry has . . .

exposed the Mormons
been featured in magazines and on TV
jam-packed revival meetings
dynamic healings
ministries to children, youth, men, women, singles, seniors
Christian counseling
a wonderful nursery and daycare
working mothers ministry
fresh contemporary music
strong youth ministry
divorce support groups
young married ministry
tanning on the beach
softball, volleyball and more
music, art and drama

My church is . . .

charismatic
traditional
contemporary
Christ-centered
Bible based
a five fold ministry
growing—new believers added every Sunday

Paul declares himself insane when forced to boast as the world does, but we have fallen in love with the insanity in the church.

(I am out of my mind to talk like this.) (2 Corinthians 11:23)

Today we consider insanity to be sane. Everything has been turned around in the church today because we have lost the message of the cross. There remains only one "I AM." No one is worth boasting about but God. Pick up a copy of your phone book and look under churches, and you will find insanity on every page, fully displayed in all of its shameful glory. Thumb through any Christian magazine and read the boasting, bragging, and appealing to the flesh. The church has forsaken the "message of the cross" and embraced the self-confidence of the world. Like the world, the church competes with other churches to win members and to make an impact in people's lives. Indeed, despite the talk about the Holy Spirit, the church relies more and more on the methods of the world to win souls for Christ. We have all but abandoned the cross that wins souls through weakness and humility. As we shall see, we consider the man or church that embraces the cross crazy, while we hold up the truly insane. In the last days, unparalleled hostility rages against the message of the cross. Because the church uses the arm of the flesh to serve Jesus, we consider the real prophet, moved of God, a "fool" and the "inspired man a maniac."

> The days of punishment are coming, the days of reckoning are at hand. Let Israel know this. Because your sins are so many and your hostility so great, the prophet is considered a fool, the inspired man a maniac. (Hosea 9:7)

Foolishness

As Paul so sarcastically writes in the passage we will now look at, "You gladly put up with fools since you are so wise!" How spiritual each church considers itself and yet they put up with "fools." Each bookstore considers itself a "ministry" while they sell the products of madmen. Each publisher thinks it serves the Christian community while using insane, worldly means to promote its products. How spiritually blind to think we can use the world's techniques, ideas, and insanity to sell our goods and yet believe we remain separate from the world. Again, ministries, seminars, bookstores, publishers, musicians, and churches gladly put up with fools. How we love to be taken advantage of by men who push themselves "forward" on us. After all, if they can promote themselves, so can we—it makes our flesh feel good to have the same freedom. The church doesn't want a Paul in its midst, who doesn't preach or promote himself, but instead reminds us that we must die to self. Christians think of themselves as so wise, yet they like being slapped "in the face." If we can get 10% off our purchases, if men can boast of themselves, if ministries can name themselves after their favorite pastor, we take the slap. We "gladly" say, "Thanks for taking advantage of us. Thanks for the insanity, it makes us feel good about our out of mind experiences."

> I repeat: Let no one take me for a fool. But if you do, then receive me just as you would a fool, so that I may do a little boasting. In this self-confident boasting I am not talking as the Lord would, but as a fool. Since many are boasting in the way the world does, I too will boast. You gladly put up with fools since you are so wise! In fact, you even put up with anyone who enslaves you or exploits you or takes advantage of you or pushes himself forward or slaps you in the face. To my shame I admit that we were too weak for that! What anyone else dares to boast about—I am speaking as a fool—I also dare to boast about. (2 Corinthians 11:16–21)

Fools preach, while boasting of how spiritual, educated, and anointed they are in God. And audiences of millions "gladly put up with fools" since they think themselves so spiritually wise and gifted. Story after story resounds from the pulpit, and we think this glorifies God. Instead of preaching the Word, we use it to tell jokes, stories, and entertain the congregation. Men tell us they can fathom the Greek and Hebrew, that they are anointed of God, and we like dumb sheep think such conduct glorifies Christ. Churches boast of how many they have reached with the gospel and we reach for our checkbooks. The church has lost its mind thinking this is sane talk in Jesus. But Paul stated that all such boasting is sinful, utterly wicked. As you read the following excerpts from 2 Corinthians 11:21–29 contrast Paul's insane talk with what happens in your church.

This is the talk of "fools" Paul shouts . . .
I am a Hebrew.
I am an Israelite.
I am Abraham's descendant.
I am a servant of Christ.
I work harder.
I have been in prison.
I have been flogged.
I have been exposed to death repeatedly.
Five times, I was lashed.
Three times I was beaten.
I was stoned once.
Three times I was shipwrecked, spending a night and day in the open sea.
I have been constantly on the move.
I have been in danger from rivers.
I have been in danger from bandits.
I have been in danger from my own countrymen.
I have been in danger in the city.
I have been in danger in the country.
I have been in danger at sea.
I have been in danger from false brothers.
I have labored and toiled.
I have often gone without sleep.
I have known hunger and thirst, gone without food and water.
I have been cold and naked.
Plus, I have started many churches I worry about.
And boy, oh-boy, do I struggle against sin.

Paul says that such boasting makes him a lunatic. For you see, we are unworthy to talk about ourselves or point to ourselves. If even Jesus said he was not good, but God alone,[1] why do we boast as if we are something? When we take on the "I am" we seek to remove God from His throne. Like Satan, we seek to set ourselves equal with God to bring all attention to ourselves. Just a quick look at the work in the church makes it easy to see the spirit of Satan. Men work for recognition and to make a name for themselves.

Reward on Earth

You might disagree with everything else in this book, but know this, the "I AM" is a position for God alone and all glory, honor and attention belongs to him. The Powerful Delusion inflames, stealing the glory from God and receiving it for oneself. Therefore, God uses Satan to send the Powerful Delusion. Who else knows how to worship self better than Satan? Satan in all his spirituality resided next to God's throne. He presents a perfect counterfeit to the message of the cross without actually requiring anyone to die to self. Satan weaves a doctrine so close to the Truth that the only way to survive is to fall in love with God. And that is exactly what God looks for, those who love Him with all their heart, mind, soul, and strength.

Men play a deadly game in Jesus. They look like they have Him in their life, but really find their life in this world. They receive their reward in the here and now, therefore they will have no reward in heaven. We must pray with the Psalmist that God "save" us "from such men, from men of this world whose reward is in this life" if we hope to escape the Powerful Delusion. Men who try to have Jesus and the world.

O Lord, by your hand save me from such men, from men of this world whose reward is in this life. (Psalms 17:14)

With each passing day, the church becomes increasingly insane as each church attempts to out-do the other churchs boasting. Pulpit after pulpit hosts drooling madmen, telling more grandiose stories each Sunday. Joke after joke, story after story fills the stages of our churches because like the world, we enjoy drawing attention to ourselves. We have fallen so far from the suffering cross of Christ in our churches that we cannot boast of sufferings, but must entertain with positive, uplifting tales. Yet, Paul declares himself a madman when he talks of the labors he accomplished, dangers he faced, and things he sacrificed. Paul claims insanity when he points to how he wrestles with sin. We, however, are more insane today, boasting of the blessings we receive.

Paul declares that he is insane to speak of anything but his weaknesses. "Are they servants of Christ? (I am out of my mind to talk like this.)" (2 Corinthians 11:23). Yet, we seem bent on promoting our churches, books, magazines, sermons, and men just as the world does.

The Madness Spreads

Truly, the church loves its insanity so much, that like the worst mentally insane, the most powerful drugs cannot stop it. We have lost sight of the cross of Christ and embraced the madness of the world. The mental illness of the world infects us. We are in a world gone mad that boasts of itself, works, labors, wisdom, accomplishments, powers and promises. We are even worse than the world for we boast like McDonald's of numbers served and fed.

Like madmen, we seek to spread our madness hoping others believe our sickness. We boast of the number of books sold in order to sell more books, so that we can boast of even more numbers sold in order to sell even more books. We no longer measure books by the truth they contain, but by what will sell. I have never met a publisher who will print a book unless they know it will sell. None have ever said, "This book will not sell, but we will print it anyway, because it has the Truth in it." The love of money, reputation, and worldly marketing infests the heart of the church. Like the Black Plague, only a few are exempt from its deadly work. Even the most conservative will reject the offense of the cross if it comes in the fullness of the Holy Spirit.

My first book entitled, *Hating For Jesus*, (Luke 14:26) which merely quoted the words of Jesus was repeatedly rejected by magazines, bookstores, and people because of the title. No one could get past the title to read the message; even among the most conservative organizations of the Christian community who pride themselves on not being like the "other" groups. Naturally, like Paul, this forced us to change the name of the book to, *The Essential Piece*.[2]

Promoting Self

We promise powerful preachers to draw the crowds and increase attendance so we can use those numbers to draw even more people to our gospel meetings and churches. We plaster our magazines with ads pointing back to ourselves and what "God" has done through us. Indeed, look at what the church shows the world. Look at the boasting, bragging, and promising that scream out everywhere. Like the world, we advertise and appeal to the flesh of man in order to "win souls."

Just as the world, we use others to promote ourselves. Yet instead of just using men and women whom God has made, we use the name of God. I say "just" because who is worse? The one who uses self to promote himself or the one who uses God to promote himself? Like the world, we use big names to promote and push forward our ministries, materials, and ourselves. We love to see pictures of ourselves on book covers, flyers, and advertisements.

We want the Christian community to notice our churches and pastors because we want recognition for ourselves. After all, who looks for "unschooled, ordinary men" to become their preachers and leaders? We want men who can boast of Ph.D.s, to rattle off stories, and entertain us, because it makes us feel spiritual to be around them. We want men capable of waxing eloquently about the Greek and Hebrew but who know nothing of hating their own lives. We only want to *feel* spiritual, not *be* spiritual. We remain unwilling to pay the price to be spiritual and suffer the pain of the cross, so we rejoice in the achievements of man. If someone were really humble and broken, knowing the holiness of God, why would they promote themselves as if they were something?

Godly Credentials

If someone actually presented a godly resume' to a church, the vast majority would consider it a very strange item. I wrote a cross-centered resume once stating my education and qualifications—an unschooled and ordinary man who spent time with Jesus (Acts 4:13). I listed my weaknesses, not my strengths, then sent it out to test the church's reaction. As you can well imagine, no job offers came in. I did however, receive one response from a church in Canada. They were very nice, but declared that God didn't want them to change their ways, but wished me the best of luck.

Earthly Recommendations

Name-dropping insanity fills the whole Christian community. Well-known, popular individuals promote and endorse books, churches, speakers, and seminars. Like the world, the church uses celebrities to market itself. The publishing world is famous for this sin. "Recommended by," the book covers declare.

Even the best of tough-talking authors and preachers fall prey to this sin. But Paul's letters never stated, "This letter is recommended by Peter." In fact, Paul states he did not resort to such worldly gimmicks to motivate individuals. He did not "need, like some people, letters of recommendation."

> Are we beginning to commend ourselves again? Or do we need, like some people, letters of recommendation to you or from you? (2 Corinthians 3:1)

What sin lies in the lap of the church, that we love to get and send "letters of recommendations"? We love to get a special speaker to our conference because it will draw in more people and give us good standing in the community. How we use each other in the name of the Lord. The popular individual uses the conference that "needs" them, while the conference leader uses the speaker to make themselves needed by the Christian community. If we really lifted up the Word and God, then why mention any big name speakers? Should not the attraction be the Word of God and not the man preaching the Word? Should people be promoted as if they were someone big and powerful in the Christian community? The bottom line is we use people and enjoy being used. We love lifting up our name and use Jesus to do it. For this reason, many ministries name themselves after the person who runs the ministry. For if we preach ourselves, men will come, but few show up when we really preach truth. Jesus said we "accept him" who comes "in his own name," because we want ourselves promoted and accepted by others. It is the sin of self-glorification.

> I have come in my Father's name, and you do not accept me; but if someone else comes in his own name, you will accept him. (John 5:43)

We borrow the glory we give certain individuals to sell books, promote seminars, and build churches. It is an abominable sin to use others' talents and popularity for our own selfish ends. Woe unto us, for the many things we promote by the sin of "recommendation." "Come hear or see this speaker!" "Buy this book because so and so likes it." It seems there is no end to this insanity. We lift men up in the church not because of what God does, but for what these men can do for us. If we really believed God works, we would not lift up men or women but just depend on God to draw people. Individuals, companies, and churches feed off and use the righteousness of others to serve themselves. We need full repentance of this selfish sin. Indeed, if true humility filled these popular individuals, they would not allow themselves to be used like that.

Each man tries to top the other in order to impress people. We are self-important mad men wanting to hear other self-important mad men puff us up in self-righteous pride. Sane men in Jesus boast of their "weaknesses." Paul declares if we must boast, we should only boast of our weaknesses. Instead, we love our "super apostles."

But I do not think I am in the least inferior to those "super-apostles." (2 Corinthians 11:5)

A Different Gospel

The Powerful Delusion presents a totally "different spirit" than the Spirit of Jesus. Jesus came forsaking self, yet the church finds itself. Jesus would not even let the demons identify Him. John the Baptist would not call himself a prophet—yet we boast and brag. Jesus lost self in the glory of God, but we use the glory of God to promote ourselves. We are not "pure virgins" because we love and embrace those who "commend themselves" and use others to promote ourselves. Eve fell prey to this sin in the Garden of Eden. Satan cleverly worked a deadly "cunning" in the church. God permits this because we no longer glory in the cross of Christ. Our "minds" have been "led astray" to vain thoughts and promotions of self. We not only "put up" with insane people in Jesus, we love them and embrace them as brothers. We call madmen our brothers and ask God to bless our insane asylums known as churches.

> But, "Let him who boasts boast in the Lord." For it is not the one who commends himself who is approved, but the one whom the Lord commends. I hope you will put up with a little of my foolishness; but you are already doing that. I am jealous for you with a godly jealousy. I promised you to one husband, to Christ, so that I might present you as a pure virgin to him. But I am afraid that just as Eve was deceived by the serpent's cunning, your minds may somehow be led astray from your sincere and pure devotion to Christ. For if someone comes to you and preaches a Jesus other than the Jesus we preached, or if you receive a different spirit from the one you received, or a different gospel from the one you accepted, you put up with it easily enough. (2 Corinthians 10:17–11:4)

We have grown so used to the "different gospel" that the true gospel is met with outright hostility or apathy. The "serpent" has worked in a very "cunning" deception by offering us all a "different spirit" than the cross of Christ. The main objective of the church is, "Will it be acceptable?" and "Will people buy it?" I can't begin to count the number of times I have been told that if I don't tone it down people will not listen.

Did you know that the music industry pays false prophets to listen to songs and make sure they offend no one? And rest assured the book publishing business has the same insanity. The church wants to make sure that the music, books, and sermons it promotes will not offend anyone, or at least not too much. Anyone can build a good reputation in the church if they preach just tough enough to be a little offensive without actually crucifying the flesh. Preach half a tough message and you will be as popular as the false prophets because many people like a tough message, it makes them feel spiritual. Preach a tough message that doesn't actually strike at self with the hammer and nails and you will be accepted by the church and heralded as a godly man.

Unfortunately, most of us can no longer discern a man acting like a "fool" in the name of God because we do not crucify, by the power of the Holy Spirit, our insanity. Until the cross has done this work in us, we cannot honestly see that we are "nothing." Paul understood his worthlessness, so why should we boast about anything? Most of us, while giving lip service to humility, know little of the fact that we are "nothing." We have refused and rejected the cross when it comes to humble us so our knowledge of humility is only one of a mocker, who mimics humble sounding words.

> I have made a fool of myself, but you drove me to it. I ought to have been commended by you, for I am not in the least inferior to the "super-apostles," even though I am nothing. (2 Corinthians 12:11)

In Our Own Name

We use "revival" to sell our name and promote our churches. In fact, you can buy revival music CDs from false revivals. They insanely advertise just as the world does, selling their merchandise. Their literature promotes their churches and themselves. Jesus did "not accept praise from men," and neither would we if we had His mind. Instead, we come in our "own name" and prove we "do not have the love of God in our hearts." Sadly, if someone really comes in the name of the Lord, we do not accept him because he does not feed our flesh. Let a man come to us in his name, using Jesus to promote himself, and we accept that with open arms and praying hands. If someone comes with purity, only lifting Jesus up, the church will "not accept" that, because they sense that they will have to lose all pride and attention for self. Ask yourself who you "accept" as godly to test how entrenched you are in the Powerful Delusion. Who do you "accept" and like the most, the "super apostles" or the "Pauls" who know the cross?

> Yet you refuse to come to me to have life. "I do not accept praise from men, but I know you. I know that you do not have the love of God in your hearts. I have come in my Father's name, and you do not accept me; but if someone else comes in his own name, you will accept him. (John 5:40–43)

The Powerful Delusion consists of men coming in their own names, let loose, and encouraged by the power of God. It is such a Powerful Delusion, few have the slightest clue that God works judgment in their life, ministry, and church. It seems to them as if God opens doors for their ministry, circumstances fall into place, blessings of peace and supply come, but only because God works a Powerful Delusion.

What self-centeredness lingers in preachers' hearts to name their ministries after themselves? I would be totally out of my mind to name this ministry, *Timothy Williams' Ministries*! Or to entitle our web site *www.timothywilliams.org*. What lunacy settles upon the body of Christ, yet even the tough talking "righteous" preachers fall prey to this insanity. Few and far between are the preachers who in heart and spirit do not preach themselves. So few men have the character of Jesus, humble enough to admit they are humble without becoming puffed up in that declaration. Such humility comes only from the mysterious power of the cross. Paul had such humility.

> For we do not preach ourselves, but Jesus Christ as Lord, and ourselves as your servants for Jesus' sake. (2 Corinthians 4:5)

In Weakness

In true humility, the fruit of a crucified life points out only things that show others our weaknesses. Sane men in Jesus speak of weak things that happen in their church and lives. But since we view insanity as normal in the church today, we consider the sane man a fool. It is one more sign that the church stands ripe for judgment. Until we return to the Holy Spirit inspired "message of the cross," having our sinful flesh crucified, the truly inspired man of God will be considered a "maniac," while the true lunatic embraced as a sane man. Let us pick up the cross Jesus has for us and sane men will once again fill our pulpits. If we must boast, it should be only of our weaknesses.

> If I must boast, I will boast of the things that show my weakness. (2 Corinthians 11:30)

Of all the things Paul could have boasted of, he chose to talk about a basket escape. The church is no longer interested in men who tell tales about a man lowered in a basket. Listen to the story Paul tells when forced to boast. He does not talk of raising the dead, numbers healed, credentials, inspiring sermons preached, dreams or visions.

> The God and Father of the Lord Jesus, who is to be praised forever, knows that I am not lying. In Damascus the governor under King Aretas had the city of the Damascenes guarded in order to arrest me. But I was lowered in a basket from a window in the wall and slipped through his hands. (2 Corinthians 11:31–33)

Do you get the picture? Imagine your church in the middle of an exciting seminar with many guest speakers. Speaker after speaker declares what God does through them and their ministries. Then up steps Paul to the pulpit. He doesn't speak of miracles, insight, visions, numbers reached, or even his special calling by God.

His speech goes something like this:

"Greetings brothers and sisters, (amen and hallelujahs are heard) I want to tell you how special God is, (*Preach it brother*). Once when God led me to preach in Damascus, He worked a mighty deliverance, (more "Amens"). This is what God did, (A quiet settles over the congregation), I was trapped in the city and men were seeking to kill me, (The drummer gets ready) and God rescued me. (Breathless silence fills the church) God allowed me to escape by getting in a basket and being lowered over the city wall."

At this point, the drummer puts down the drumsticks at this boring story. While the congregation would politely say "Praise God," they would never invite this dull speaker to their church again because they thought him boring and ineffective.

Recognizing Insanity

As the old top ten song goes, "They're coming to take me away ha-ha, he-he, ho-ho . . . to the funny farm. They're coming to take me away." No one in the church comes to take away insane leaders and put them in straight jackets.

It reminds me of my college days when the world tutored me in its wisdom. While earning the foolishness of a degree in psychology, I learned of a case study concerning insane asylums. In this study, a group of psychology students checked themselves into the asylum to see if the staff of psychologists and psychiatrists could discover that they were really sane. The staff could not detect the students, but the patients in the institution saw through the students.

All the great wisdom of the staff provided no insight to distinguish the sane from the insane. Only those who understood their own mental illness could recognize those who had nothing wrong. In the same way, those who love God must come to see their own insanity in order to discern the sane in God. The cure for insanity in the church is to honestly admit what areas of our flesh are drawn to insane men. Only the cross of Christ, crucifying a man, can help us see that reality.

We must allow the cross of Christ to crucify our thoughts and flesh in order to be sane in Jesus. In order to connect to the head, who is Jesus, our own heads must die. After all, no body has two brains ruling it. That would be utter chaos and insanity. Exactly the point of Colossians 2:19.

> He has lost connection with the Head, from whom the whole body, supported and held together by its ligaments and sinews, grows as God causes it to grow. (Colossians 2:19)

When we lose "connection with the Head" the church begins to behave in ways that reflect man's insanity rather than the humility of Christ. Only as we allow the mind of Christ to rule us will the church become sane again. God lays a clear choice before us. Either we learn to "hate" our thoughts or continue to fellowship with the insane. We must come before the Lord telling Him we "hate" our way of thinking. We must allow a crown of thorns to torment our thoughts so that we loathe them, and come to wince at our opinions.

If we want to possess the mind of Christ, which is one of true righteousness, then we must fall in humility before the Lord and admit we have behaved like insane men. Like patients in the mental institution, we must humble ourselves and admit our insanity before we can see who and what constitutes sanity in Jesus. This is hard to do because going to church today resembles committing oneself to a mental institution, rather than entering a place of worship. The very people who are supposed to help us are more deluded than ourselves, for they use Scripture to make self appear and feel spiritual. Everyone boasts of numbers saved, people reached, money tithed, and how spiritual their preachers are in the Lord. It is as if the mental patients all sit around and see who can top each other. The church has become a house full of insane individuals boasting of their gifts, works, and labors for the Lord.

This love of insanity in the church opens wide the door for all manner of arrogant and prideful men to rise up in the pulpits. We cannot even begin to start a work without first thinking of how we will promote it. Even the few good preachers and saints left today are beginning to question what little bit of sanity they have left. For if you hang around insane men long enough you begin to doubt your sanity. After all, "bad company, corrupts good character," (1 Corinthians 15:33). Let us come out of the insane asylums and pick up our crosses.

Chapter 3

NUMBERS MADNESS

"Go and count the Israelites from Beersheba to Dan. Then report back to me so that I may know how many there are." (1 Chronicles 21:2b)

"Over 1,000,000 sold!" the ads boast and brag. From software to books, from cars to music, numbers matter to the world. And when a true Christian's belief challenges someone, the retort is that "no one else believes this." Indeed, if I had a dollar for every time someone said, "Well, no one else sees it that way," I would be a very wealthy man.

McDonald's restaurants boast of the number of hamburgers they sell. Under the golden arches a statement boldly proclaims "billions served." This sinful desire to boast of numbers reflects in the church today. Like psychiatrists who make up names for illnesses, I call it the *McDonald's Factor*.

Boasting as the world marks a church ripe for judgment. God will judge the madmen in His sanctuary. All who boast in the way the world does will face the full fury of God's punishment. Not every McDonalds continues to post their numbers sold but the church latched onto counting and built upon the sin.

McNumbers Factor

In 1988, when I first preached on this mental illness in the church, we gave away free sermon tapes on this topic. In order to make the point we went to several McDonalds in our town and requested cheeseburger wrappers. Each restaurant kindly gave us some of the yellow paper wrappers. We then cut them up into four sections and wrapped each tape to look like a cheeseburger. Needless to say, this was a great way to make the point, until the district McDonalds office in our town got wind of it. They didn't like their sin revealed anymore than the church. We received a rather nasty letter, not only from the local office, but also from the world headquarters for McDonalds in New York City. They sent a letter back from their lawyers demanding we no longer use their name and materials. It seems the district manager had forwarded all of our materials, including the sermon tape to the big wigs in New York. God used this to preach the gospel all the way to the top. It would have made a very interesting court case, but we submitted to their request and renamed the sermon "The McNumbers Factor."

Again, what the world does, boasting of billions served, the church embraces with a full, sinful heart. Because of this love for the flesh and its way, fools now preach from the pulpits. As a church, we must realize that if we act like the world, then something is drastically wrong.

A church's desire to talk of how many they save or serve in the Lord comes straight from the heart of Satan. It is pride displayed in all kinds of false humility. It is insanity about what we have done and will do in the Lord. What started out as little attendance boards and gold stars has grown to full-blown insanity. For this reason, the scripture below declares that such boasting "comes not from the Father but from the world."

> Do not love the world or anything in the world. If anyone loves the world, the love of the Father is not in him. For everything in the world—the cravings of sinful man, the lust of his eyes and the boasting of what he has and does—comes not from the Father but from the world. (1 John 2:15–16)

God's Anger

When God becomes angry at the pride in the church, He allows Satan to rise up against us. In Scripture, this judgment began in two different ways.

> Satan rose up against Israel and incited David to take a census of Israel. (1 Chronicles 21:1)

> Again the anger of the Lord burned against Israel, and he incited David against them, saying, "Go and take a census of Israel and Judah." (2 Samuel 24:1)

One states that "the anger of the Lord burned against Israel" while the other declares "Satan rose up." Both are true. Israel became proud and God's angered began to burn as He saw what hid in the heart of each Israelite. God planned to bring in the light the things that smoldered in their hearts. So too, in the last days God sends a "Powerful Delusion" involving miracles performed by Satan in order to cause our sin to surface so that we might repent or be judged.

The great idol loved in the church today is numbers. God's Word, Jesus' name, and calls of revival are used in order to increase attendance. The church loves increased membership, making it the sign of a growing church. This golden calf allows all manner of sins to come flooding into the church.

The church has forgotten the hard lessons David learned. His command to go and count ended in the death of 70,000 Israelites. Now there is a number to remember. Indeed, it would end with God standing over Jerusalem to "destroy" it. The seemingly benign command to just see "how many there are" is a grievous sin in the eyes of the Lord, for it is the pride of man rearing its ugly head.

> Again the anger of the Lord burned against Israel, and he incited David against them, saying, "Go and take a census of Israel and Judah." So the king said to Joab and the army commanders with him, "Go throughout the tribes of Israel from Dan to Beersheba

and enroll the fighting men, so that I may know how many there are." But Joab replied to the king, "May the Lord your God multiply the troops a hundred times over, and may the eyes of my lord the king see it. But why does my lord the king want to do such a thing?" The king's word, however, overruled Joab and the army commanders; so they left the presence of the king to enroll the fighting men of Israel. (2 Samuel 24:1–4)

It is a sad time in a church when God must use Satan to discipline His saints. When we cannot be cleansed by Scripture alone, or convicted by God's watchmen, God resorts to using Satan through the Powerful Delusion. The only problem is, for most it will not end the way it did for David. How little conviction of sin the church feels today about counting. Woe unto them that do not see this as discipline but as a blessing. One has to wonder if any real conviction remains. Where are the men who will stand up in churches and ministries to declare counting "repulsive" in the Lord? Who feels what God feels?

> But Joab did not include Levi and Benjamin in the numbering, because the king's command was repulsive to him. (1 Chronicles 21:6)

Many defend counting by retorting that God recorded that 3,000 people were added to the church at Pentecost. They use the blessing of God as a license to sin, and twist the Scriptures to fit their own selfish ends. The recording of 3,000 saved at Pentecost declared God's mercy. For what the Law took away, mercy restored. At the coming of the Law, 3,000 died. God's Pentecost demonstrates restoration at the coming of His Spirit. In both places of Scripture, the wording matches.

> The Levites did as Moses commanded, and that day about three thousand of the people died. (Exodus 32:28)

> Those who accepted his message were baptized, and about three thousand were added to their number that day. (Acts 2:41)

The hundred and twenty mentioned in Acts 1:15 points to the weakness of man. Of how small the church was and how large it would become in one day, by the power of God, not by the power of man's advertising. It is a count done by the hand of God which points to the weakness of man. Not a group of leaders presumptuously claiming a successful evangelic campaign. Let us be sure of one thing, the desire to count in the church is a vile sin before the Lord. Indeed, the Old Testament records David's lesson so that we might not do what they did.

> This command was also evil in the sight of God; so he punished Israel. (1 Chronicles 21:7)

David's Repentance

Let every church everywhere repent and not do what they did, for the command to count is "evil in the sight of God" and He will punish for it. Let all who have counted become like David.

> Then David said to God, "I have sinned greatly by doing this. Now, I beg you, take away the guilt of your servant. I have done a very foolish thing." (1 Chronicles 21:8)

Let the godly "beg" the Lord to take away the stain of this guilt. Let them pray and repent so their garments are spotless when they enter the gates to stand before the Lord. To be sure, God must punish people who commit such a sin, for their pride must be broken. Yet, He will forgive if we repent. Be wise like David and seek out God's seers. Choose to fall into the hands of the Lord as His seers point out the sin that blinds you. Seek out men who will show you no favoritism and can help you repent. Don't play the old self-righteous game of saying, "Oh, I prayed about it and God forgave me. He said it was ok." Get the heart of David and learn what constitutes godly sorrow.

> The Lord said to Gad, David's seer, "Go and tell David, 'This is what the Lord says: I am giving you three options. Choose one

of them for me to carry out against you.'" So Gad went to David and said to him, "This is what the Lord says: 'Take your choice: three years of famine, three months of being swept away before your enemies, with their swords overtaking you, or three days of the sword of the Lord—days of plague in the land, with the angel of the Lord ravaging every part of Israel.' Now then, decide how I should answer the one who sent me." David said to Gad, "I am in deep distress. Let me fall into the hands of the Lord, for his mercy is very great; but do not let me fall into the hands of men." (1 Chronicles 21:9–13)

This is no normal sin. Let conviction burn within every ministry, church, and individual who has ever counted. For all who have known what their left hand is doing, deep repentance will be demanded.[1] Let preachers and elders fall face down before the Lord in sackcloth. For the angel of the Lord stands above your church to strike it. The presence of God comes to a church that talks of numbers, but He is there to destroy. How many worship leaders declare the truth when they declare, "The presence of the Lord is in this place." They are just too dull to see that God is there to judge, not to bless. The Powerful Delusion hovers over your congregation while the leadership commits great sins in the name of the Lord. Let each leader take it personally upon themselves to repent openly before the whole congregation. To say with David, "These are but sheep." May each man take upon himself the full weight of this sin.

> So the Lord sent a plague on Israel, and seventy thousand men of Israel fell dead. And God sent an angel to destroy Jerusalem. But as the angel was doing so, the Lord saw it and was grieved because of the calamity and said to the angel who was destroying the people, "Enough! Withdraw your hand." The angel of the Lord was then standing at the threshing floor of Araunah the Jebusite. David looked up and saw the angel of the Lord standing between heaven and earth, with a drawn sword in his hand extended over Jerusalem. Then David and the elders, clothed in sackcloth, fell facedown. David said to God, "Was it not I who ordered the fighting men to be counted? I am the one who has sinned and

done wrong. These are but sheep. What have they done? O Lord my God, let your hand fall upon me and my family, but do not let this plague remain on your people." Then the angel of the Lord ordered Gad to tell David to go up and build an altar to the Lord on the threshing floor of Araunah the Jebusite. So David went up in obedience to the word that Gad had spoken in the name of the Lord. (1 Chronicles 21:14–19)

Ransom

One of the great leaders in this sin today is the publishing industry. It sets the trends in the church. Indeed the numbers insanity is even on the back of children's books. Woe unto us because we cause little ones to stumble. Better to have a millstone tied around our neck than to infect them with the spiritual illness of insanity. The absurdity in such insanity is that it is not needed. I personally enjoy reading a certain series of children's books because the stories are straight forward, clean, and to the point, and I am over 45 years old. But this publisher boasts more than 55 million sold on the back cover! What an unnecessary claim. People would buy them because of their quality without such a bold statement. But we love our insanity as much as we love the story of Jesus. This demonstrates the Powerful Delusion in its child-like simplicity. If we play the "numbers sold" game, then the best selling worldly novel must also be of God, and so must the largest religion in the world. But we know the truth, that the number of books sold does not mean the Lord blesses it. They advertise this way to motivate people to buy the book and to brag about themselves. How powerful this delusion is that from the most lofty of ministry, to the smallest of children's books, insanity runs rampant.

Let all return in obedience to God, and understand that when counting happens, each person must pay a price. Each individual in the church who permits themselves to be counted should "pay" to the Lord "a ransom for his life at the time he is counted." In other words, each Christian should have a full understanding of the seriousness and danger of counting members in the name of the Lord. At that very moment of counting the ransom must be paid. Each church member must see the pride in themselves that desires to be counted and be part of a growing ministry or movement.

> Then the Lord said to Moses, "When you take a census of the Israelites to count them, each one must pay the Lord a ransom for his life at the time he is counted. Then no plague will come on them when you number them. (Exodus 30:11–12)

May we all be like the first church, growing and living in the fear of the Lord, and not count because of holy fear of God.[2] David, whose heart we sing about, felt "afraid" of the Lord's sword and could not even pray to the Lord. For this sin of counting not only exalts our ego and pride, but it also causes the angel of the Lord to raise the sword against us.

> But David could not go before it to inquire of God, because he was afraid of the sword of the angel of the Lord. (1 Chronicles 21:30)

Let men and women who love God pay the price of repentance today. For if we want to be sane in Jesus, then the price must be paid in full. Let the godly who have committed this sin "insist on paying the full price" of repentance. We must fully repent of the love of numbers and remove the leaders from the pulpits and off the committees who will not repent. Let us instead rejoice in whatever fruit God allows in our lives as Habakkuk 3:17–18 states:

> Though the fig tree does not bud and there are no grapes on the vines, though the olive crop fails and the fields produce no food, though there are no sheep in the pen and no cattle in the stalls, yet I will rejoice in the Lord, I will be joyful in God my Savior. (Habakkuk 3:17–18)

We must give thanks just as fully whether we have large numbers or no one in our churches.

Chasing Jesus Away

Be sure of this, any church that commits the sin of counting drives Jesus away. All the miracles, joy, and movements of the Holy Spirit reveal nothing more than the Powerful Delusion doing its deadly work. For counting causes Jesus to leave us, and if Jesus has "left" He is not in our miracles. Or if the miracles came from Him, He will renounce the churches that do not repent. As the Scripture below shows us, Jesus leaves a counting church.

> The Pharisees heard that Jesus was gaining and baptizing more disciples than John, although in fact it was not Jesus who baptized, but his disciples. When the Lord learned of this, he left Judea and went back once more to Galilee. (John 4:1–3)

Like the Pharisees of old, whenever a doctrinal debate arises, men retort with what they consider important. Nearly every time someone wants to debate with me about Scripture they always jump to the all important questions: "How has your church grown?" and "How many go to your church?" As if how large a church we have would settle the doctrinal concern. Notice in the passage below that an "argument" came up about ceremonial washing between John the Baptist's disciples and some Jews. But when they approach John, they don't discuss the doctrine in question. They pounce on the issue of numbers! They appeal to John's pride by saying, "Jesus is baptizing, and everyone is going to him."

> An argument developed between some of John's disciples and a certain Jew over the matter of ceremonial washing. They came to John and said to him, "Rabbi, that man who was with you on the other side of the Jordan—the one you testified about—well, he is baptizing, and everyone is going to him." (John 3:25–26)

Empty Sheep Pens

Numbers don't mean a thing. Obedience to God's Spirit and doing God's will is all that matters. God may call you to support a missionary, church, or ministry that doesn't win a single convert for years, but the numbers shouldn't matter. God looks for faithfulness, not numbers. Faithfulness to His word and will. After all Noah and Jeremiah didn't win a single convert, but continued to maintain truth.[3] Indeed, Abraham died with a very small "congregation" although he had been promised innumerable descendents. But to think such a thought in today's church is considered insane. Loony folks fill our pulpits, seminaries, and publishing companies today. Not only do the numbers inflame the pride in men, we miss the point that longsuffering is blessed in the Lord's sight. For the same love that "won a large number of disciples" was also manifested when just "a few men became followers."[4]

Counting is the opposite of love and therefore God fiercely opposes it. Impersonal governments count, and the anti-Christ will make sure everyone is counted and controlled. Counting uses people while love pours itself out no matter what the number. Love is not self-seeking and counting arises from a self-seeking heart that wants others to know our accomplishments. Like David let us "insist" on paying the "full price" of repentance. How many people fall short when it comes to the matter of repentance. At the first symptom of guilt, they pray, claim a promise, yet go on their merry way to hell. There must be a death to the sin and a full measure of repentance, sometimes lasting months.

> But King David replied to Araunah, "No, I insist on paying the full price. I will not take for the Lord what is yours, or sacrifice a burnt offering that costs me nothing." (1 Chronicles 21:24)

Repentance that doesn't "cost" is "worldly sorrow" and cannot save anyone. Though it is "sorrow," coming with tears and prayers, it will never cleanse the sinner or lead to a place of forgiveness. "Worldly sorrow" is wasted sorrow over sin that only leaves "regrets" over wasted prayers, tears, and worship.

> Godly sorrow brings repentance that leads to salvation and leaves no regret, but worldly sorrow brings death. See what this godly

sorrow has produced in you: what earnestness, what eagerness to clear yourselves, what indignation, what alarm, what longing, what concern, what readiness to see justice done. At every point you have proved yourselves to be innocent in this matter. (2 Corinthians 7:10–11)

What will it be for us? Lukewarm worldly sorrow that attempts to cleanse itself from sin, or the full measure of hot godly sorrow over sin? Sadly, for many in the church there is no sorrow at all.

The Holy Spirit draws individuals to Jesus in spite of the offense of the cross. In the quest for numbers, the church has removed the offense and replaced it with entertainment, motivational skills and enticements. Jesus declared that when He is "lifted up" He will "draw all men" to Himself.

But I, when I am lifted up from the earth, will draw all men to myself." (John 12:32)

It is the Holy Spirit's work to draw men, not the responsibility of men. Men are to plant or water, but God gives the harvest. None of the efforts of the man who "plants" or "waters," and I quote God here, "is anything."

I planted the seed, Apollos watered it, but God made it grow. So neither he who plants nor he who waters is anything, but only God, who makes things grow. The man who plants and the man who waters have one purpose, and each will be rewarded according to his own labor. (1 Corinthians 3:6–8)

As John the Baptist declared, "A man can receive only what is given him from heaven."[5] Sadly, most numbers that fill the pews are a result of men's efforts, not the Holy Spirit's work. It is easy to tell this is true because the way someone became a "Christian" was not in spite of the offense of the cross, but through the persuasive words and programs of outreach committees.[6] Many millions who confess Jesus as Lord have a faith that results from "men's wisdom" that came with "wise" preaching.[7] Only when we have declared the offensive message of Jesus, as He works it through us, can we honestly speak of someone being born by the power of God. Without the offense of the cross present, we are no different than that world that wins converts to their causes, opinions, and beliefs.

Men reject the true offense of the cross for one major reason— they love their ministries more than Christ. All they can see is their ministries. The offense of the cross crucifies a man to such attitudes. Without it we remain helplessly selfish in our work for the gospel of Jesus. We are to "lift up" the offensive cross of Jesus, to "clearly portray" Jesus as crucified. In the desire for greater attendance we justify the removal of the offense by saying, "The message of the cross is offensive, but we are not be offensive." Such excuses bear no resemblance to Scripture or the life of God's true preachers. Yes, we can be offensive in our flesh, but we can also err by removing the offense of the cross because it does not suit our purposes, plans, and goals.

> Before your very eyes Jesus Christ was clearly portrayed as crucified. (Galatians 3:1)

We must always "clearly portray[ed]" Jesus "as crucified" in every sermon, work, project, and publication. This is why in all that Paul preached and did he "resolved" always to focus on the offensive cross of Christ.[8] By the power of the Holy Spirit, we must present an offensive cross to each man, woman and child. If this was true for the mother of Jesus, it will be true for everyone else.[9] No one is exempt from the offense of the cross, except false Christians.

Chapter 4

GREAT THINGS MADNESS

Not so with you. Instead, whoever wants to become great among you must be your servant, and whoever wants to be first must be slave of all. (Mark 10:43–44)

"God has great plans for your life," is the mantra chanted by the church today to prospective individuals invited to become Christians. Churches full of insanity, and those touched by the illness, preach that great things await new believers. Unfortunately, without the cross, such promises become temptations or bribes luring people into a false hope. When we offer God without the message of the cross, we make men demons. Demons use the things of God to enrich themselves. We tell others that God wants to fulfill their dreams because we no longer really believe man is totally wicked. And since we do not feel our wickedness, we believe our dreams, plans, prayers, and hopes are worthy. But the message of the cross tells us that man deserves punishment, and that is why Jesus died. Only those who admit, by the power of the Holy Spirit, that they "deserve" the cross in their life will escape the Powerful Delusion.

Take for example the two thieves crucified with Jesus. Both desired salvation, but their hearts were as different as light and darkness.

One of the criminals who hung there hurled insults at him: "Aren't you the Christ? Save yourself and us!" But the other criminal rebuked him. "Don't you fear God," he said, "since you are under the same sentence? We are punished justly, for we are getting what our deeds deserve. But this man has done nothing wrong." Then he said, "Jesus, remember me when you come into your kingdom." (Luke 23:39–42)

The key difference between the two thieves is that one wanted salvation *from* the cross while the other took up his cross freely admitting that he deserved it. Only those who admit, accept, and fully endure the pain of the cross in their lives will be in paradise with Jesus. Any other kind of preaching insults the glorious gospel of Jesus and mocks the reason for His death. Until the preaching returns to a complete acceptance that man is "worthless," there is no chance of escaping the Powerful Delusion. For at the heart of the Powerful Delusion lies the belief that something good resides in man.

God's Grief

Preaching today exclaims the fact that we are "fearfully and wonderfully made." It tells us we are made in God's image and of value in His sight. Messages often proclaim that Jesus died for us because of our value to God. When we remove the message of the cross, such truths become twisted and abused to a selfish and prideful end.

Consider carefully that you hold no value in God's sight. God regretted ever making you, or in the words of Genesis 6:6, "The Lord was grieved that he had made man."

When the Lord looks at Timothy Williams, He is "grieved" and "filled with pain" that He made me. While it is true that God "wonderfully" made me, equally true is that mankind ruined itself. We were perfectly made, but have perfectly ruined ourselves. From the cutest of babies to the kindest of grandmas, we fill God with "pain." We have gone off in search of many schemes and made ourselves utterly contemptible in His sight.

> This only have I found: God made mankind upright, but men
> have gone in search of many schemes. (Ecclesiastes 7:29)

We have made ourselves "worthless" and of no value to God
by embracing sin. We need to meditate on the passage below until
God gives us insight into our true nature. Read this to yourself,
then read it to those you love until all fall prostrate before the
Lord. Read it to your pastor until each and every sermon he preaches
reflects and rings of this truth. The more we know this truth, the
richer God's mercy and love will flow in our lives. Indeed, those
who feel forgiven of much will love much.[1] However, if we deny
our worthlessness, how can we be forgiven? For if a man thinks he
is correct on something, he will think God falsely accuses him.
When we feel worthless, we will let Jesus crucify us. We will understand for certain that the only good in us is Jesus, for we "no
longer live" and His goodness dwells in us.[2] Look at what Paul
says about himself and us.

> As it is written: "There is *no one* righteous, *not even one*; there is
> no one who understands, no one who seeks God. *All have turned
> away*, they have together *become worthless*; there is *no one who
> does good*, not even one." "Their throats are open graves; their
> *tongues practice* deceit." "The poison of vipers is on their lips."
> "Their mouths are full of cursing and bitterness." "Their feet are
> swift to shed blood; ruin and misery mark their ways, and the
> way of peace they *do not know*." "There is *no fear of God* before
> their eyes." (Romans 3:10–18 emphasis added)

Our very lives, thoughts, actions, and worship of God rise as a
stench in His nostrils. Until we are convinced of this by the Holy
Spirit, and not just paying lip service to the concept, we remain
prime targets for the Powerful Delusion. Self always wants to think
it possesses something good, and that is exactly what the anti-
Christ will say. He will tell us there is something good in man.
Until we realize that Jesus did not die for us because of our value,
but because of who He is, we will not have the humility to accept
the cross in our lives. Every time the cross seeks to crucify us, we

will object that we do not deserve such treatment from God. Until we can fully rejoice in the fact that "nothing good" resides in our "sinful nature," we will never experience the freedom and deliverance from sin. Until the church repents of the insanity of desiring great things, the preaching of the cross will remain full of human wisdom and powerless to deliver anyone from hell.

> I know that nothing good lives in me, that is, in my sinful nature. (Romans 7:18)

When Jesus speaks of us being more valuable than birds, He means in relationship to God's attributes in us, not man's worthiness. As when someone speaks of something of value to them because of invested time and memories, but not in terms of actual worth. This understanding gives us the correct interpretation of Luke 12:24 and Romans 3:12.

False Promises

We can promise only one great thing to a new Christian—God will make them a "servant of all." The cross will empty them of selfish pride, self-glorification, self-exaltation, and self-serving attitudes. The church must tell new converts that the abundant life is found in losing one's life. But the Delusion twists the abundant life to mean success and fulfillment in this world. Demons confirm the lie by whispering that to lose your life means you will receive blessings from God. This hellish lie seeks the living God for what it can get. Satan twists the truth by saying if you give up the things of this world, you will get it all back.

Every new Christian or future disciple, should be told the great thing God will do for them is to make them "last." Not only because they deserve this, but it is what heaven in like—everyone becoming the slave of others. Everything about the church, the preaching, the songs, the ministry work, and the books should work toward this goal. It should encourage, bless, and point the way to the cross so that every person claiming to be a Christian becomes the "very last."

Sitting down, Jesus called the Twelve and said, "If anyone wants to be first, he must be the very last, and the servant of all." (Mark 9:35)

When we promise individuals great things in God, we stand with Satan. For Satan tells us we can be "like God" with others serving us, but Jesus tells us to become a slave to others. The church today talks about being "gods," powerful like God, and even seeks to find self-esteem in Jesus' name. True enough, as stated before, we are "wonderfully made," but so was Satan. And when Satan noticed how wonderfully God made him, he wanted to use that truth for his own selfish ends, and became the Devil. Like the Devil, millions are taught in every church to be proud of their beauty in God. Satan whispers in the church's ear that it is the "model of perfection, full of wisdom and perfect in beauty." He whispers and the false prophets shout that they are "anointed," "ordained," and "blameless," but have not heard from God.[3]

This "wisdom," however, is "corrupted" because the demon of self has not been crucified and the "splendor" of our works, projects, and noble ministries has blinded us to our true condition. It has blinded us to the time period in which we live. It is not time to be lifted up, but to fall to the ground and die to self.[4] Either we fall to the ground or God will throw us down to hell. Just as God threw Satan "to the earth," so will He cast out the unrepentant believers.

"Son of man, take up a lament concerning the king of Tyre and say to him: 'This is what the Sovereign Lord says: "'You were the model of perfection, full of wisdom and perfect in beauty. You were in Eden, the garden of God; every precious stone adorned you: ruby, topaz and emerald, chrysolite, onyx and jasper, sapphire, turquoise and beryl. Your settings and mountings were made of gold; on the day you were created they were prepared. You were anointed as a guardian cherub, for so I ordained you. You were on the holy mount of God; you walked among the fiery stones. You were blameless in your ways from the day you were created till wickedness was found in you. Through your widespread trade you were filled with violence, and you sinned. So I drove you in disgrace from the mount of God, and I expelled you, O guardian cherub, from among the fiery stones. Your heart became proud on account of your beauty, and you corrupted your wisdom because of your splendor. So I threw you to the earth; I made a spectacle of you before kings. (Ezekiel 28:12–17)

The Cross Removed

Our "wisdom" has become "corrupted" because the cross is no longer lifted up in order to crucify self. Indeed, most people have no need for such a cross. They reason that since Jesus paid the price, men should not have to die to self. Just as selfish desires corrupted Satan's beauty, so has sin perverted man's. Both worship self, and only by returning to the suffering of the cross can we become free from the judgment that Satan received. Peter tells us just as Jesus had to suffer on the cross to be finished with sin, so must we suffer. Only those "who have suffered in" their bodies are "done with sin."

> Therefore, since Christ suffered in his body, arm yourselves also with the same attitude, because he who has suffered in his body is done with sin. (1 Peter 4:1)

Only after we suffer with Christ can we speak of a "result" of righteousness in someone's life. We like to quote with Paul "I have been crucified with Christ." However, unlike Paul there is no proof in our lives that the Holy Spirit has done the crucifixion work.[5]

When the church, however, promises great things and all that is required is "faith," there is no need for the cross. It is a false human faith as when the world speaks of having faith in themselves or someone. Unless we return to same "attitude" as Christ, God will send a delusion in our life so that when the anti-Christ arrives we will gladly take the mark. It will seem like the most reasonable, logical, and godly thing to take the mark of the beast to those who have refused to suffer with Christ against sin in their life.

Feel Good Gospels

Because the Powerful Delusion has worked its insanity so well, the church hardly notices that the cost of being a disciple of Jesus has almost disappeared. Whenever the cost is mentioned, it is quickly diluted with vain promises of self-glory. The contest rages between feel-good gospel calls and the bad-feeling gospel calls. People often say, "I get a bad feeling about your message." Feelings have become the measurement because we worship the feelings of our flesh rather than a living God. The gospel calls in most churches today, which you can find printed on the back cover of many Bibles, all reflect the Powerful Delusion. The just ask-Jesus-in-your-heart, "Romans Road"[6] programmed prayers we teach men to recite reflect not the gospel call of Jesus, but the wide road that leads to hell. We tell hungry, searching people to expect great things for themselves and to selfishly call upon the name of Jesus. No wonder the gospel call reduces down to a selfish prayer of just asking Jesus in your heart to accept Him as your own little personal Lord and Savior. After the prayer, the person goes out to find their blessing. No one tells new converts that they must pass through "many" hardships in order to enter heaven. The "good news" of the Bible tells us to preach that men must "go through many hardships to enter the kingdom of God." Those who know they deserve a cross in their life receive this as good news. But to those ripe for the Powerful Delusion, such gospels are anything but good news. Notice what the Apostle Paul preached as the "good news" of the cross every where he went.

> They preached the good news in that city and won a large number of disciples. Then they returned to Lystra, Iconium and Antioch, strengthening the disciples and encouraging them to remain true to the faith. "We must go through many hardships to enter the kingdom of God," they said. (Acts 14:21–22)

Paul said we "must" (note well the word "must") go through many hardships to enter the kingdom of God." In other words, no one can enter heaven without having gone through many hardships, struggles, and refinement. This was no simple wide-road gospel call, this was the real thing. It was the way Jesus walked and the way we must all walk.[7] We should not preach that great things await Christians except the "pure joy" of facing trials.

If you took a survey among Christians today and asked them, "What gives you joy in Jesus?" The answer would be all His blessings, maybe even homes and a well put together life and family. Rarely would anyone say, "Oh, the pure joy I find in Jesus is facing hardships. That is the highest and purest joy in the Lord." Very few would answer according to James 1:2, "Consider it pure joy, my brothers, whenever you face trials of many kinds."

The feel good gospel call promises great things for everyone, helping them to discover their potential in Christ, while the bad-feeling gospel call scares people. Many who listen to our sermons often comment that they get a "bad feeling" even though everything sounds correct. Indeed, they wish they could find something wrong to ease their bruised consciences and provide an excuse not to obey. That bad feeling comes from the cross trying to do its work, but the Powerful Delusion and its preachers claim it is from the devil. What a twist to view the cross of Jesus as something so hellish. But what can you expect when the church teaches that any conviction is condemnation, quoting "There is no condemnation in Jesus." They confuse conviction with condemnation because they have hard hearts and do not want to give up their sins. The response results from the teaching that we can be free in Christ apart from being crucified with Christ. When crucifixion with Christ is twisted to mean you get your blessing, fear naturally occurs because conviction is surpressed. The result ends in rebellion against what God only meant as a blessing of conviction. Like spoiled children we scream, "condemnation." Just like a child that yells, "You don't love me!" when a good parent attempts to discipline him.

A good example of this twisting took place at a conference where a keynote speaker took the message of the cross, which had been presented to him, and preached it very logically. He twisted the message to say, "You will get what you want when you give up what you want." So the bottom line of his message was that we deny ourselves so that self might get its desires—the Powerful Delusion in its best form.

Long gone is the message of John the Baptist that calls the "crowds" who come to hear his sermons a "brood of vipers!" John asked seekers why they came to his church and who qualified them to "flee from the coming wrath?"[8] The cross disappeared and we never tell individuals who have served God that they only did their "duty" and do not deserved to be blessed.[9] The Powerful Delusion takes people to Jesus and instructs them on how to ask for great things. Like the Apostles they come in false humility saying, "Teacher, we want you to do for us whatever we ask."

> Then James and John, the sons of Zebedee, came to him. "Teacher," they said, "we want you to do for us whatever we ask." "What do you want me to do for you?" he asked. They replied, "Let one of us sit at your right and the other at your left in your glory." (Mark 10:35–37)

The Powerful Delusion preaches that insanity is holy before the Lord, so go ahead—ask, claim, and walk in whatever great thing you desire. God must react like King Achish, "Am I so short of madmen that you have to bring this fellow here to carry on like this in front of me? Must this man come into my house?"[10] How mad the church has become as it requests and promises one great thing after another. Like the Apostles, we have no idea what we are asking.

> "You don't know what you are asking," Jesus said. "Can you drink the cup I drink or be baptized with the baptism I am baptized with?" "We can," they answered. Jesus said to them, "You will drink the cup I drink and be baptized with the baptism I am baptized with, but to sit at my right or left is not for me to grant. These places belong to those for whom they have been prepared." (Mark 10:38–40)

As individuals ask for "glory," the Powerful Delusion tells them to glory in their self-seeking prayers instead of instructing them to prepare for the "cup" of the Lord. The same cup that Jesus drank, which produced prayers so intense that he sweated "drops of blood."[11] A "cup" so painful that even Jesus asked if it could pass by Him.[12] We can no longer point people to a Christianity that has an offensive cross[13], but instead tell them to ask and claim what great thing they want, and God will give it to them.

Holy Fear

The feel-good gospel is man's attempt to avoid the cross of Christ that crucifies the flesh, and instead makes the flesh feel spiritual. For example, when Jesus called Peter, James, and John, He promised them a great work and commission in God, yet they experienced the cross, not a worldly kind of promotion or favor.

> Then Jesus said to Simon, "Don't be afraid; from now on you will catch men." (Luke 5:10)

Also note that they felt "afraid." Jesus did not flatter them into the kingdom but humbled and convicted them of their unworthiness to follow Him. When the Holy Spirit first calls someone to Jesus, He often terrifies them. Just back up a few verses and see how Peter first reacted to the call of God in his life.

> So they signaled their partners in the other boat to come and help them, and they came and filled both boats so full that they began to sink. When Simon Peter saw this, he fell at Jesus' knees and said, "Go away from me, Lord; I am a sinful man!" (Luke 5:7–8)

As God's blessings flowed into Peter's life, he cried out to Jesus to leave him. Indeed the cross bids us to leave our blessings behind in order to follow Jesus to Jerusalem to die. We are called to be like Jesus, who set out to make himself poor that others might be rich.[14]

Peter's pride was shattered and he felt deeply his unworthiness to follow Jesus. Jesus first presented Peter, James, and John with the offense of the cross before speaking of great things. They had to drink from the cup of the cross for years before the "blessings" would become a reality. But when those blessings came, they were for the sake of others. For they had learned the truth that it is "better to give, than to receive."[15]

Today when we lead others to Jesus, we look at their talents, likes, and dislikes and tell them what areas would make them a good Christian. There is even a test that rates what spiritual gifts a person has in the Lord. We have forgotten the cross that tells us nothing good lives in our flesh. Think about it, if we are dead to self in Christ, how can a dead man have talents? Believers are not taught that all their dislikes, desires, and talents must be utterly and completely put to death in order to be used by God. Jesus spent three years teaching Peter this lesson. At the end of Peter's lessons in the way of the cross he wanted nothing to do with the calling and blessing that God had for him. This is ever the way of the cross. When God finally crucifies a man, the self-confidence and vainglory die, and therefore fleshly motivation no longer remains in the work God calls us to.

Godly Motivation

Jesus had to urge Peter on to fulfill the calling God had for his life after the cross had been clearly presented. He had to ask Peter three times, "Do you love me?" in order to remove the excuses. The first time Jesus wants to know if Peter loves him more than things, "more than these." With all the prosperity around us, we can ask ourselves no greater question than if we love *Jesus* more than "these" things. Do we love Jesus more than the *things* of Jesus? The Powerful Delusion will put that question to the test.

Jesus asked Peter two more times, "Do you love me?" Jesus wanted to urge Peter to willingly "feed" and "take care" of God's sheep. Jesus comes to each of us with the call to follow Him. He asks, "Do you love me?" over and over to some of us. But we love our grand plans, our ministries, our work, and our lives more than Him. For all our bravado, we are not slaves of all, but promoting our ministries and lives.

> When they had finished eating, Jesus said to Simon Peter, "Simon son of John, do you truly love me more than these?" "Yes, Lord," he said, "you know that I love you." Jesus said, "Feed my lambs." Again Jesus said, "Simon son of John, do you truly love me?" He answered, "Yes, Lord, you know that I love you." Jesus said, "Take care of my sheep." The third time he said to him, "Simon son of John, do you love me?" Peter was hurt because Jesus asked him the third time, "Do you love me?" He said, "Lord, you know all things; you know that I love you." Jesus said, "Feed my sheep. I tell you the truth, when you were younger you dressed yourself and went where you wanted; but when you are old you will stretch out your hands, and someone else will dress you and lead you where you do not want to go." Jesus said this to indicate the kind of death by which Peter would glorify God. Then he said to him, "Follow me!" (John 21:15–19)

We never become indignant like Peter screaming, "Yes, Lord!" and then go out to become the "slave of all." Instead, we go out in the name of the Lord to get all the blessings we possibly can and motivate others do the same. The Powerful Delusion uses others for its own gain and comfort. If you answer "yes" to Jesus, rest assured you will be led like Peter, "where you do not want to go."

> I tell you the truth, when you were younger you dressed yourself and went where you wanted; but when you are old you will stretch out your hands, and someone else will dress you and lead you where you do not want to go." (John 21:18)

Gone is the Peter who in human zeal would die for Jesus. The man who proclaimed at the Last Supper that he would die with Him, yet in the end did not even want to work for his Lord. He went off fishing when he should have been preaching. He rightly felt unqualified and unfaithful for such work. Self, with all of its pride, had been broken. This is the wonder of the cross in a man's life. But it is a slow, painful, and hard process that few are willing to endure. Everyone wants their quick, enormous blessing and a whole host of false churches of all styles offer such messages. Everyone wants to expand their ministries, but it is all for self.

Even as Jesus restored and admonished Peter to come out of himself enough to "feed" and "take care" of God's sheep, Peter still would be led where he did "not want to go." The cross does not stop until we are fully and completely dead. Those who serve God go where they "do not want to go" and must go all the way.

We need to remember that the sum of the Christian Spirit-led life is that we do not do what we want to do. The Powerful Delusion blesses what we want to do, but the cross of Christ crucifies our desires. Each and every day we are in the middle of a "conflict" and our surrender determines the outcome. The false prophets like to preach that God's way is whatever we want. Their attempt at preaching is to make this sound holy and to scratch itching ears.[16] The true gospel puts us in the middle of a conflict.

> For the sinful nature desires what is contrary to the Spirit, and the Spirit what is contrary to the sinful nature. They are in conflict with each other, so that you do not do what you want. (Galatians 5:17)

To preach a Jesus that demands we go His way rather than our own is totally contrary to the insanity message. The insane message encourages the glorification of man's will and does not tolerate a true cross. Whenever God promises a commission to any man, self and flesh must be crucified. The insane preachers remove this part of the message of the cross. The attempt is to try and get man's will to appear like God's will, or as Jesus put it, "whitewash tombs" that only appear clean. "On the outside" it may "appear" we perform "righteous" works for God, but our "inside" has not been put to death by the cross.

> "Woe to you, teachers of the law and Pharisees, you hypocrites! You are like whitewashed tombs, which look beautiful on the

outside but on the inside are full of dead men's bones and every-thing unclean. In the same way, on the outside you appear to people as righteous but on the inside you are full of hypocrisy and wickedness." (Matthew 23:27–28)

Think about Moses. By the time it was God's will for Moses to fulfill his calling he wanted nothing to do with it. God had so deeply removed self, with all of its zeal that Moses didn't want anything to do with his blessing.

But Moses said, "O Lord, please send someone else to do it." Then the Lord's anger burned against Moses and he said, "What about your brother, Aaron the Levite? I know he can speak well. He is already on his way to meet you, and his heart will be glad when he sees you. (Exodus 4:13–14)

Indeed, Moses resisted to the point of angering the Lord. The cross does this to a man. It burns self out to the point of disobedi-ence and stubbornness. The insanity message lifts men up in self-importance and offers them the blessings of God without the cross and they run in pride to do the work. Just notice how so many love to talk of their ministries and labor. Pride and self ooze out from every pore. It is easy to see the cross has not been allowed to work. One can only weep as new converts are promised minis-tries, gifts, and positions of authority, causing them to fall under the same condemnation as Satan.

He must not be a recent convert, or he may become conceited and fall under the same judgment as the devil. (1 Timothy 3:6)

Comfortable Leadership

Over the years, churches have placed many young men in high positions who now preach and lead in churches. Because these vast multitudes of men and women never experienced the suffer-ings of the cross, today prideful, self-centered people lead the church. It is not hard to see why so many embrace insanity and

74

reject the sanity of the cross. For when they are confronted with their long-standing sins of self and pride, they use all their authority and power to silence the one rebuking them.

So much insanity fills the halls of the churches that we consider a little appearance of self-denial in Jesus enough to qualify people for work in Christ. We have forgotten the lesson of Gideon. Though humble and used mightily by God, Gideon ended his life ensnaring Israel in sin, all because he grabbed a little bit for self when doing God's work. Gideon had "one" little request—only one "earring." How often we are hindered and ensnared over "one" small request to please self. Of course the people gladly "give" this blessing of self to Gideon. After all, they had been blessed and wanted a leader who was willing to allow them to have blessings for themselves as well.

We can relate to this kind of leader. We hire teachers with whom we can find fault, because that makes us comfortable around them. We don't want them to be totally wicked, but want them to feed just enough of self to make us relax about our sins. Indeed, for all the moaning and groaning about bad leadership in the church, in reality, most people would not last ten minutes under godly leadership that is "aiming for perfection."[17]

> And he said, "I do have one request, that each of you give me an earring from your share of the plunder." (It was the custom of the Ishmaelites to wear gold earrings.) They answered, "We'll be glad to give them." So they spread out a garment, and each man threw a ring from his plunder onto it. The weight of the gold rings he asked for came to seventeen hundred shekels, not counting the ornaments, the pendants and the purple garments worn by the kings of Midian or the chains that were on their camels' necks. Gideon made the gold into an ephod, which he placed in Ophrah, his town. All Israel prostituted themselves by worshiping it there, and it became a *snare* to Gideon and his family. (Judges 8:24–27 Emphasis added)

Today these "snares" are not small, or few or far between. In fact, we view them not as snares but as blessings sent from God.

No wonder it is called a Powerful Delusion. Pastor after pastor, church after church and ministry after ministry exchange "gold rings" with one another in order to set up shrines to themselves and their ministries. Pastors encourage individuals to look for their gifts, blessings, and promises that will enshrine self in their lives.

The Highest Blessing

Truly God has great plans for our lives, but they do not include the blessing of self. He plans to transform us into His holiness. In order for God to achieve His goal of sharing His holiness with us, we must be disciplined. Disciplined with a painful cross in our lives.

> Moreover, we have all had human fathers who disciplined us and we respected them for it. How much more should we submit to the Father of our spirits and live! Our fathers disciplined us for a little while as they thought best; but God disciplines us for our good, that we may share in his holiness. No discipline seems pleasant at the time, but painful. Later on, however, it produces a harvest of righteousness and peace for those who have been trained by it. (Hebrews 12:9–11)

For sure this discipline is not "pleasant at the time, but painful." We lie when we tell young converts that God has great plans for their lives, if we do not warn them that much discipline and pain awaits them first. Of course, "later on" it will produce "a harvest of righteousness," but they need to persevere before they can talk about holiness. But only those "trained by it" can honestly claim this holiness. Most just endure the time of discipline without learning anything from it. They are not "trained" by the cross but endure the pain because they know they must. They do not submit to the pain of the cross for righteousness sake, but only so they can go to heaven or obtain a blessing. When we endure with this selfish motive, we are not ready for heaven, because we have not been "trained" by God's righteousness. We remain wicked individuals without transformation. Sure some people might hang on the cross, but refuse to die. They hang to get blessings from God, not to give up their lives.

How amazing that so many people know for certain how God will bless someone when they come to Christ. Before them stands sin-soaked individuals, loaded with vile motivations, corrupted characters, defiled consciences and the church tells them God has great plans for them. How does the person telling them know God's plans? Yes, they are great plans if you consider the way of the cross to be God's highest blessing for a man's life. For God to make a Job out of someone is a tremendous blessing. Does anyone ever declare to a new convert, "God has great plans for your life. He is going to make a Job out of you."? Or that they may be like a Stephen who will not live long? Such thoughts are abhorrent to the church today and we see no glory in such statements. The only type of insight shared is worldly blessing and comfort in order to attract people to church. The insanity in the church will not speak of being "sawed in two" or living in "holes in the ground."

> They were stoned; they were sawed in two; they were put to death by the sword. They went about in sheepskins and goatskins, destitute, persecuted and mistreated—the world was not worthy of them. They wandered in deserts and mountains, and in caves and holes in the ground. These were all commended for their faith, yet none of them received what had been promised. (Hebrews 11:37–39)

Hebrews commended these Christians "for their faith." They remained, however, "destitute" and "none of them received what had been promised." Until a church feels comfortable telling someone that God's plan might include being "destitute," they are infected with the sinful illness called insanity. In order to become sane in Jesus, we must return to His gospel that drives a man in very serious contemplation to "sit down and estimate the cost." Instead, like worldly game shows where self wins prizes, we tell people to "come on down" and get Jesus. Or like a form in a catalog to order goodies, we sign the back form in a Bible to order

Jesus as our personal Lord and Savior. Jesus did not say "come on down," He said "sit down."

> "Suppose one of you wants to build a tower. Will he not first sit down and estimate the cost to see if he has enough money to complete it? (Luke 14:28)

Losing Our Lives

As Jesus declared the great blessings of God, He also revealed that those blessings come only through the cross. Like criminals, we use anyone, even God to get what we want. The church reflects the world and the distinction is almost non-existent anymore. No real cost is counted, therefore we have no need to "sit down" and measure the cost of the cross. Jesus warned them to "sit down" and think about what this powerful and dynamic cross would do in their lives. The feel-good-promise-anything-gospel-calls certainly do not drive anyone to "sit down" and "estimate the cost." Indeed many who read this will wonder what cost to even consider.

I discuss how to count the cost in my book entitled, *Even The Demons Believe*[18], but let me touch upon it here. The only thing we should promise when leading someone to accept Jesus as Lord and Savior, is that God will take their life and crucify it. All their hopes, dreams, pleasures, pains, ideas, thoughts, opinions, time—everything will slowly be taken and crucified. The great thing God has called all men to do is to "hate" their own life, to become nothing. Without this hatred for one's life no one, I repeat, no one has the eternal life of Jesus in them.

> The man who loves his life will lose it, while the man who hates his life in this world will keep it for eternal life. (John 12:25)

Hating our life in this world is the greatest call God has for anyone calling themselves a Christian. Whether our calling resembles Job, David, Paul, or Stephen, the cross will take all of a man and put him to death. After all, no greater blessing awaits us than to be emptied of ourselves and filled with God's holiness. He who has a noble heart considers it a blessing to get rid of such a vile thing as oneself.

The abundant life has been twisted to mean a successful life in this world. The blessed life without the cross becomes a demon's best weapon to blind someone toward Jesus. For the words about losing one's life have been robbed of all power and saltiness. Men can then agree with the words and state that they live it, but the meaning and power is lost and they are deluded to the truth. Under the influence of the Powerful Delusion, losing your life becomes something twisted and perverted. One only loses his life to get something. Self is not killed but goes underground so that it can seize its life in the name of Jesus. Self wraps itself in the garments of self-righteousness—but underneath lies a raging wolf.

A Servant

At the fall in the garden, we wanted to grab onto our blessing. In the last days God will allow the Powerful Delusion to give us power to grasp and bless ourselves. However, the cross is the opposite of this, as you might expect if you have read this far. Jesus' life showed us the way to death of self and the road we must all walk if we desire salvation. Our "attitude" should be like Jesus, who being in very nature God, did not grasp onto or claim equality with God and His blessings.

> Your attitude should be the same as that of Christ Jesus: Who, being in very nature God, did not consider equality with God something to be grasped, but made himself nothing, taking the very nature of a servant, being made in human likeness. And being found in appearance as a man, he humbled himself and became obedient to death—even death on a cross! Therefore God exalted him to the highest place and gave him the name that is above every name, that at the name of Jesus every knee should bow, in heaven and on earth and under the earth, and every tongue confess that Jesus Christ is Lord, to the glory of God the Father. (Philippians 2:5–11)

Jesus "made himself nothing" and became in "very nature" a "servant." He did not wear a mask mixed with false humility. In heart and spirit He literally made Himself a servant, a slave—nothing. A slave does not claim great things. Nor does a slave feel he should; he has no rights. He knows he is a slave and will not be in charge of anything until Jesus' second coming. Slave means you do not do what you want or enjoy. Even more than that, being the slave of all means you spend all your energy blessing others. No time, comfort, or fun is yours, rather you live to make others comfortable.

Jesus died having never sought a personal blessing. Everything He sought after, prayed about, and worked toward benefited others. Jesus is the example we must follow of losing our life to find life in God.[19] Few are those who have the attitudes of humility in their heart that "we are unworthy servants; we have only done our duty."

> "Suppose one of you had a servant plowing or looking after the sheep. Would he say to the servant when he comes in from the field, 'Come along now and sit down to eat'? Would he not rather say, 'Prepare my supper, get yourself ready and wait on me while I eat and drink; after that you may eat and drink'? Would he thank the servant because he did what he was told to do? So you also, when you have done everything you were told to do, should say, 'We are unworthy servants; we have only done our duty.'" (Luke 17:7–10)

This nothingness was a lifelong matter while Jesus remained in this world. Not until after He died on the cross, could Jesus talk of being "exalted." For He certainly was never exalted here on earth. Likewise, now is the time for us to be humbled and broken and to suffer against the sin in our lives. We will not fully live the resurrected life until Jesus returns. Now is our time to "fall to the ground" so that when Jesus returns, He will find something to resurrect. It is the greatest folly to claim forgiveness, or to be told to "forgive yourself" when God has not declared it. What we claim does not save us, but whether God has forgiven us. A man can claim salvation all day long yet be hell bent for destruction.[20] When Jesus returns He will only save those who "die" in Him right now. If you have not died to self there will be nothing for Jesus to make alive.

> I tell you the truth, unless a kernel of wheat falls to the ground and dies, it remains only a single seed. But if it dies, it produces many seeds. (John 12:24)

The Powerful Delusion claims its blessing in this world and seeks to avoid the cross at all costs. For the true Christian the world offers no reward. Like Abraham you might die with only a congregation of four; like Noah you might only win your family; like Jeremiah you might not win a single repentant sinner; or finally, like Jesus, you might die on a cross with everyone thinking you failed. Like Abraham, you die knowing the world is yours, but not possessing a single inch of land. Only those "obedient unto death," death on a "cross," will find themselves exalted in God's kingdom. For this reason Jesus proclaimed that many who appear to be first in the Lord in this world are really last in heaven. Think of it, ministries well known and popular today, if they were of God at all, will mostly likely be last.

> But many who are first will be last, and the last first." (Mark 10:31)

Finally the good news, the great thing to promise someone just beginning to follow Jesus is that God will make them "nothing." So tell them not to even strive to "grasp" great things for themselves in the name of Jesus. To promise more only allows the Powerful Delusion to work its deadly lie. We must remember that Jesus "made himself nothing," (Philippians 2:7). This is the goal of the cross that God places on a man's back. It hangs over his life everyday, every hour of every day, and yet is the easy yoke of God.[21]

Think about Jesus. He left the treasures in heaven, gave up all comfort, did not settle in here, died to make others happy, and made Himself poor and suffered while on earth. We must emulate Jesus without grumbling[22] that the message is too hard. Like Jesus we will be used by others but must keep loving to the very end. The footsteps we follow lead us to become "nothing," not become great.

> "Not so with you. Instead, whoever wants to become great among you must be your servant, and whoever wants to be first must be your slave—just as the Son of Man did not come to be served, but to serve, and to give his life as a ransom for many." (Matthew 20:26–28)

We are to lose all for Jesus, just as Jesus lost all for us.

> Whoever finds his life will lose it, and whoever loses his life for my sake will find it. (Matthew 10:39)

In this world we will be the lowest of losers. The world will view us as losers and, in all reality, we are losers by the world's standards. In fact, we become the "scum" of the earth. The great thing God has in mind for you is to let you become the "scum of the earth." God rejoices and angels sing when you are willing to become the "refuse" of the world, and that when the world comes to take your property, you will accept it with all joy. You will help them carry your things out, because you have found it a joy to be a loser for Jesus.

> You sympathized with those in prison and joyfully accepted the confiscation of your property, because you knew that you yourselves had better and lasting possessions. (Hebrews 10:34)

When you seek to make a new disciple for Jesus, point them to Him and then to one of the great saints of old like Paul. Pray with them that they too will be blessed of God to become losers, trash, refuse, and the scum of the world.

> Up to this moment we have become the scum of the earth, the refuse of the world. (1 Corinthians 4:13)

Think of those who followed Jesus. They lost families, occupations, money, homes, reputations, careers, fun, pleasure, rest, sleep, influence, power, educations, retirement, lands, and even health. "I die every day—I mean that, brothers . . ." Paul declares in 1 Corinthians 15:31. In fact, it was because of an "illness" that Paul preached the message of the cross. How many treat the foolishness of the message of the cross with "contempt" and "scorn." Such individuals are easy pickings for the Powerful Delusion.

> As you know, it was because of an illness that I first preached the gospel to you. Even though my illness was a trial to you, you did not treat me with contempt or scorn. Instead, you welcomed me as if I were an angel of God, as if I were Christ Jesus himself. (Galatians 4:13–14)

If you hear it preached we are to be winners in Jesus right now, know that you are staring straight into the face of the Powerful Delusion. True Christians will become losers increasingly with each passing day. Great things do not face the true disciple of Jesus. That is the bribe of the Powerful Delusion to pull multitudes away from the living God. Just as Jesus died having lost all the world, so too we win only by becoming losers in the world. Our "reward" and any positions of authority will not happen until Jesus returns.

> "Behold, I am coming soon! My reward is with me, and I will give to everyone according to what he has done." (Revelation 22:12)

The more we lose now, the greater our reward will be when Jesus returns.[23] We need to pray with David that God deliver us from false Christians whose "reward is in this world." (Psalm 17:14) For it is the man who finds his life, even though it be in the name of Jesus, that will lose it for all eternity. The richness of our blessings are with Jesus in heaven right now and we must await His return before they will fully be ours. We are "blessed" "in the heavenly realms with every spiritual blessing," not blessed with the things of this world.

Praise be to the God and Father of our Lord Jesus Christ, who has blessed us in the heavenly realms with every spiritual blessing in Christ. (Ephesians 1:3)

True enough we will "inherit the earth," but not until Jesus creates a new heaven and earth.[24] It is not great things that await Christians, but a cross that will cause us to lose all. Christians, praise God, are the greatest losers of all in this world. This is the way of the "daily" cross.

Then he said to them all: "If anyone would come after me, he must deny himself and take up his cross daily and follow me. For whoever wants to save his life will lose it, but whoever loses his life for me will save it. (Luke 9:23–24)

Chapter 5

AUTHORITY MADNESS

The prophets prophesy lies, the priests rule by their own authority, and my people love it this way. But what will you do in the end? (Jeremiah 5:31)

The church and "priests rule by their own authority," they are mad with the spiritual illness we will label authority madness. How loudly the church proclaims the following, but what will they "do in the end?"

- We are priests in God.
- Not losers, but winners!
- We are gods in Christ.
- Men, take authority over your destiny.
- Women, rise up in the authority you have in Jesus.
- We are god-like in our power and authority.
- It is all ours in Jesus, the world and the heavens.
- We take authority over finances, health, lands, and homes.
- We take this city for God.

Without the cross, these declarations become the work of demons inspiring men to covet what is not rightfully theirs. The authority madness that grips the church causes people to use their "mouths" to "lay claim to heaven" as they "take possession of the earth." These "Christians" talk of having authority over everything, from the spiritual realm to the physical realm. They preach that they are in charge and therefore "people turn to them and drink up waters in abundance." For who doesn't like the temptress words declaring that we just need to claim our rightful place, fulfill our calling, and take authority over all?

> For I envied the arrogant when I saw the prosperity of the wicked. They have no struggles; their bodies are healthy and strong. They are free from the burdens common to man; they are not plagued by human ills. Therefore pride is their necklace; they clothe themselves with violence. From their callous hearts comes iniquity; the evil conceits of their minds know no limits. They scoff, and speak with malice; in their arrogance they threaten oppression. Their mouths lay claim to heaven, and their tongues take possession of the earth. Therefore their people turn to them and drink up waters in abundance. (Psalms 73:3–10)

Boasting that you have the fullness of the resurrected life unveils a truly insane man. This is our time of discipline, refinement, and testing to see who will endure the sufferings of Christ out of love for God, not the time for taking authority.[1] Now is our time to lose all, fall to the ground, pick up our daily cross and become a slave of all. The resurrected life will not be ours until we are resurrected with Jesus. Indeed, Jesus looks for those willing to be like Him here on earth and therefore worthy of being like Him in heaven.

The promise of great things with a feel-good gospel call has created a warm environment for the sin we will examine in this chapter. We will touch on the sin of rebellion against positions assigned by God. If you have jumped to this chapter without reading the previous ones, you may want to go back to the beginning before pressing on. Without an understanding of the cross and the insanity of the Powerful Delusion, this chapter will make little sense. For the sin we are about to examine can only happen when the insanity has reached its peak. The final point will be when the anti-Christ exalts himself in the temple, because he treasures pride and self-glorification. This sin of taking authority over all is disguised in false humility, but easily seen by those crucified with Christ and lifted up from the world.[2]

The Deepest Insanity

The fullness of this insanity manifests in the accepting and embracing of women pastors within the church. For men literally have to be insane to accept a woman pastor and call it a blessing. Only madmen find insanity to be something good. Nothing short of a demonic spirit encourages and blesses women in the pulpit. Demons revolted at the position God made them for and sought a higher one. They did not "keep their positions" just as women have rejected their purpose.

> And the angels who did not keep their positions of authority but abandoned their own home—these he has kept in darkness, bound with everlasting chains for judgment on the great Day. (Jude 1:6)

Man's pride encourages haughtiness in women. For a long time men strove to be something in the church, and grabbed on to more than what God permitted. The "selfish ambition,"[3] slowly unleashed among men in the church, has now reached the lap of women. Many years ago a slow rejection of the humility of the cross and a striving to make a name for self began in the church. With all the means available to promote oneself, the love of most has grown cold. Men resorted to gimmicks and advertising in order to gain recognition in the church. Men rejected the positions appointed by God in order to establish themselves as someone important in the church. The judgment is nearly complete, for many women today seize the moment to be something in the name of the Lord. This is a most sinister form of rebellion with the Lord's name tacked on.

The church flatters and excites people's pride so much, that it considers godly and holy to have women abandon their "own homes." Indeed, women have literally abandoned the home in order to fulfill their "calling in the Lord." The family is falling apart not because of worldly influences, but because women have abandoned the home, their God ordained position and calling.

Proverbs 31

> Likewise, teach the older women to be reverent in the way they live, not to be slanderers or addicted to much wine, but to teach what is good. Then they can train the younger women to love their husbands and children, to be self-controlled and pure, *to be busy at home,* to be kind, and to be subject to their husbands, so that no one will malign the word of God. (Titus 2:3–5, emphasis added)

Women view the teaching to "be busy at home"[4] as some benign and menial command and abandon their rightful positions by the droves. The church no longer has enough older women to teach younger women how to be busy at home and to love their husbands.[5] All have run after the world seeking to claim their place in the world for Christ.

All the way back to Miriam, before the Law, women led the other women. In any church a woman should never lead men in worship. Whether worship includes dancing, singing, or song leading women are only permitted to lead women.

> Then Miriam the prophetess, Aaron's sister, took a tambourine in her hand, and *all the women followed her*, with tambourines and dancing. (Exodus 15:20, emphasis added)

Teachers quote Proverbs 31 declaring that the woman of noble character must have had a job to purchase a "vineyard" and thus nullify the Word of God with the Word of God. In other words, they quote Scripture back to Jesus for their own selfish interest and become like Satan who quoted Scripture for his own gain. In order to avoid this sin, we must crucify our self-centered interests and live out all Scripture. Only in doing so can God fulfill both scriptures for a woman to be "busy at home" and to buy a vineyard out of her earnings. Churches preach that there is "no male or female" in Christ, but use Truth for selfish ends.[6] They twist this Scripture to give women freedom to take upon themselves the position men should hold. If this were the correct interpretation then when a man becomes a Christian he should be capable of giving birth, after all, there is no male or female in Christ. The truth is that Christ gives salvation to all, no matter what gender or race, but each person should occupy their God ordained position. As we shall see, to desire anything else is to align oneself with demons and Satan himself.

God created woman as a helpmate to man, in order to free man to be the priest of the home. Women, however, want to be priests not only of the home but also of the church. They have rejected the blessings of God and do not continue in faith and love. No longer do women feel the need to be "saved through child birth."

> But women will be saved through childbearing—if they continue in faith, love and holiness with propriety. (1 Timothy 2:15)

Women now feel free from the command to remain at home and instead preach rebellion while claiming freedom in Christ. The same sin happened in the garden when Eve believed she would not die if she disobeyed God. Likewise, women preachers declare they will not die if they disobey God's true calling.

Churches, magazines, books, and sermons all encourage women to rebel and fulfill themselves in the name of Jesus. The same judgment that awaits demons applies to women who fill the pulpits in our churches. Just as there are demons in the dark right now, so too darkness engulfs the church concerning this sin. The command is clear. It is a sin for a women to "teach or have authority" over a man.

> I do not permit a woman to teach or to have authority over a man; she must be silent. (1 Timothy 2:12)

The Garden

What Paul wrote had nothing, absolutely nothing, to do with a local problem in that church. Paul wrote this because of how God created the universe and the events that took place in the Garden of Eden.

At the beginning, God created the stars, planets, and the vast array of the universe. The planets were set in motion and the very fabric of the universe so tightly woven, that nothing could interfere with God's plan.[7] Everything was in its proper place. The Creator made everything in His perfect order so that each new thing could exist. God in His infinite wisdom created man before woman. For this reason, Paul gives the command that a woman cannot "teach" or "have authority over a man."

For Adam was formed first, then Eve. (1 Timothy 2:13)

What utter foolishness to even assert that Paul wrote this command because of something cultural. Paul declares correctly that the Lord does not permit woman to teach or have authority over man because God made Adam first.

God did not create Eve to be a teacher to man. He meant for Adam to lead her, just as man was taught by God. In the Garden of Eden, Eve rebelled against this arrangement, and rejected the home God made for her. This is the second reason Paul gives for the command.

And Adam was not the one deceived; it was the woman who was deceived and became a sinner. (1 Timothy 2:14)

Paul did not write about a cultural matter in regards to this teaching, but stated the facts surrounding the fall. The downfall of mankind happened only one way and the effects apply to mankind in every culture, country, and land. Eve sinned and was deceived first concerning the Word of God, therefore she is not permitted by God to "teach" or "have authority over a man." It is important to understand that Eve ignored and disobeyed God before man did. As the insanity of pride and self-glorification become the norm in the church, women rise to ignore what God clearly stated. Women take the blessing of Adam for themselves a thousand times everyday in churches everywhere.

> The woman said to the serpent, "We may eat fruit from the trees in the garden, but God did say, 'You must not eat fruit from the tree that is in the middle of the garden, and you must not touch it, or you will die.'" "You will not surely die," the serpent said to the woman. "For God knows that when you eat of it your eyes will be opened, and you will be like God, knowing good and evil." When the woman saw that the fruit of the tree was good for food and pleasing to the eye, and also desirable for gaining wisdom, she took some and ate it. She also gave some to her husband, who was with her, and he ate it. (Genesis 3:2–6)

In verse three, Eve acknowledges with clear insight that "God did say" not to eat from that tree—she willfully rebelled just as women do today. She could not see through the serpent's cunning schemes, because her flesh desired to rule over man—to be as God—above all, to be noticed, and to occupy a position not her's. It is rebellion against God's perfect plan. Only a satanic heart desires to fulfill a calling not of God.

Therefore the serpent went to the woman first to destroy God's plan and will. The serpent knew if he could get the woman to sin, everything would turn backwards. Men would follow women instead of God, women would lead and God's perfect will thrown into sin and chaos.

Wisdom from Satan

Eve ate the fruit of the "knowledge of good and evil." So too the rebellious women filling our pulpits today appear full of wisdom and "knowledge." Their wisdom, however, does not come from the Holy Spirit but is confirmed by Satan and worked in the audiences by demons. It isn't godly wisdom but the inflamed wisdom of pride and rebellion quoting Scripture. It is wisdom that comes from a forbidden fruit.

Indeed the only reason these women seem so wise is that men are so spiritually inept. It is not hard to appear awe-inspiring to a first grader. If men were not so spiritually dumb they would not be so easily led away by women preachers. There is no kind way to put it. Truthfully, any man with even a small amount of spiritual wisdom would see through it all.

As we saw earlier, Satan quoted Scripture to Jesus, so these women use Scripture to promote themselves. God has released the Powerful Delusion, allowing and confirming the lie that women can have authority over men—sometimes with signs, wonders, and spiritual feelings. God allows Satan to authenticate the lie he started in the Garden of Eden because men and women refuse to accept the Truth. Today "movements of the Spirit" endorse and encourage the breaking of this command. For when a woman pastor declares she can feel the presence of God in what she does, she tells the truth. God allows a presence to be felt and permits her to believe it is the Living God so that the Powerful Delusion can march forward.

Women preachers, like the fruit in the Garden, appear "pleasing to the eye." On the surface, our flesh doesn't see anything wrong with women being in positions of authority or teaching men. In fact, just as the fruit gave wisdom to Adam and Eve, a woman pastor can impart wisdom to a congregation. But make no mistake about it, her wisdom does not come from the Holy Spirit, but from the Powerful Delusion working deadly insanity.

Deborah's Heart

We must pause a moment and mention Deborah "leading Israel" in the book of Judges, for those desiring to justify the sin of women preachers do so by pointing to Deborah. While it is true that Deborah did "lead" Israel, they miss the whole point.

> Deborah, a prophetess, the wife of Lappidoth, was leading Israel at that time. She held court under the Palm of Deborah between Ramah and Bethel in the hill country of Ephraim, and the Israelites came to her to have their disputes decided. (Judges 4:4–5)

Deborah led Israel because God could not find any men willing to take charge. Her story took place during a period of judgment because of the sin of the Jewish nation. During the time of Judges, Israel found itself in great need of righteous men and women. In fact the book of Judges said that "everyone did as he saw fit."[8] We live in the last days when everyone decides what they consider to be good in the Lord, and they do as they see fit. Deborah on the other hand wanted the men of God to repent and lead Israel. She knew God's perfect plan and burned with a passion to see her people return to obeying the Lord. Because Barak was not willing to take leadership, God tried to use Deborah to shame him. She declares, "because of the way you are going about this, the honor will not be yours, for the Lord will hand Sisera over to a woman."

Sadly the same is true today. Like Barak, men cannot even be shamed into leadership. They are insane like Barak, willing to accept shame as a blessing from God.

> Barak said to her, "If you go with me, I will go; but if you don't go with me, I won't go." "Very well," Deborah said, "I will go with you. But because of the way you are going about this, the honor will not be yours, for the Lord will hand Sisera over to a woman." So Deborah went with Barak to Kedesh. (Judges 4:8–9)

Deborah had God's heart and longed for men to lead. When Israel won the battle, she burst into song. Look carefully at what she sang. Listen well to the love song of her heart concerning her leadership. Feel the passion she had in her soul for the Word of God.

> On that day Deborah and Barak son of Abinoam sang this song: "When the *princes* in Israel take the lead, when the people willingly offer themselves—praise the Lord! (Judges 5:1–2)

The song in Deborah's heart sang that men, the "princes in Israel take the lead." Be assured of one thing, if Deborah had her way, she would be busy at home in God's perfect will. Deborah had no desire at all to lead or make judgments in Israel. She knew that was man's place. A spirit of self-glorification did not motivate her, but an honest desire to glorify God. She had no sinful motive to fulfill her calling and destiny. Her heart was with the "princes."

> My heart is with Israel's princes, with the willing volunteers among the people. Praise the Lord! (Judges 5:9)

If you know a church where a woman is the pastor and there are no qualified or willing men to lead, have them contact us. We will quickly provide a qualified and "willing" man to lead that church.

God's Judgement

A church or nation ripe for God's wrath will have women in positions of leadership. It is one of God's signs of the coming destruction and judgment on the world and against a nation. Just take a quick look around. What do you see? Children in rebellion and women leading. Children run the home and women no longer stay at home. The false church encourages women to seize the day and fulfill their lives in the name of Jesus. God will arise and judge a church, ministry, organization, magazine, or book for preaching rebellion against God. As the Scripture below declares, God will "rise to judge" those who "turn you from the path" by having "women rule over them." No wonder "youths oppress" our nation, while women forsake their positions not only in the home, but in church as well.

> Youths oppress my people, women rule over them. O my people, your guides lead you astray; they turn you from the path. The Lord takes his place in court; he rises to judge the people. (Isaiah 3:12–13)

Women in a position over men in the church, many times placed there by man, become "guides" that "lead you astray." Insanity grips leaders, who have lost connection with the Head and preach a gospel not of Jesus. They cannot see their sin because they remain loaded down with boasting of themselves, flattery, and works done in the name of the Lord but for themselves. In fact, often those who believe that women can rebel against this command will justify it by pointing to all the good works and wisdom accompanying a specific woman leader. The very fact they protest this way demonstrates that their hearts overflow with insane thoughts. They don't realize that the Powerful Delusion is a test to see if we really love God. The Powerful Delusion comes with men and women preaching in God's name, and their prayers are answered. But they preach of another Jesus, not the Jesus of the cross. Millions of Christians and churches fail the "test" everyday. Women preachers are "gods" the church has "not known" and it is the false church that seeks to undo this past commandment.

The Great Delusion is Deuteronomy 13 worked out on a grand scale. It is the coming of prophets with great power preaching a Jesus that is not really Jesus. The "testing" is this: will we listen to preachers who proclaim a false Jesus, though it comes with miracles, "wonders" and "dreams," or will we "love" God? The Great Delusion comes with all these elements, the elements of the Scripture below. God sent this test among the Jews of the Old Testament and He is sending one within the church today.

> If a prophet, or one who foretells by dreams, appears among you and announces to you a miraculous sign or wonder, and if the sign or wonder of which he has spoken takes place, and he says, "Let us follow other gods" (gods you have not known) "and let us worship them," you must not listen to the words of that prophet or dreamer. The Lord your God is testing you to find out whether you love him with all your heart and with all your soul. (Deuteronomy 13:1–3)

The Powerful Delusion is God's way of "testing" us. It takes the refining fire of God to reveal to the angels who loves God and who doesn't.[9] Those who love God will overcome the insanity and "purge" the evil of women leaders in the church. Without this cleansing it doesn't matter what you believe—only actions count before the Lord. Actions reveal the difference between sheep and goats.[10]

With sadness one can see each church and denomination slowly giving way to the insanity that sweeps across the world. Little by little small compromises occur, even in denominations that acknowledge this to be true. Soon everyone will be like the churches that fully embrace women in leadership in the church. Indeed, there will come a time when all men will hate the true church.

Sign of Authority

To fully repent of this sin requires that woman wear a "sign of authority" on her head while in church.

> For this reason, and because of the angels, the woman ought to have a sign of authority on her head. (1 Corinthians 11:10)

Not only is it a sin for women to "teach or have authority over a man," but "she must be silent" in church.

> I do not permit a woman to teach or to have authority over a man; she must be silent. (1 Timothy 2:12)

God has arranged the church as He sees fit, and part of that arrangement says that "women should remain silent in the churches." Indeed, the Scriptures declare that it is "disgraceful for a woman to speak in church."

> For God is not a God of disorder but of peace. As in all the congregations of the saints, women should remain silent in the churches. They are not allowed to speak, but must be in submission, as the Law says. If they want to inquire about something, they should ask their own husbands at home; for it is disgraceful for a woman to speak in the church. (1 Corinthians 14:33–35)

As pointed out before, this is not some cultural command Paul gave. Most individuals write off this command as a cultural thing or some powerless nonsense. Theologians and commentaries claim

Paul told the Christian women not to dress like prostitutes and theorize about the local situation. Nothing could be further from the truth.

Ask yourself if this sounds like cultural comments from Paul. Read why Paul said that every woman in church should wear a "sign of authority."

> Now I want you to realize that the head of every man is Christ, and the head of the woman is man, and the head of Christ is God. (1 Corinthians 11:3)

Not Cultural

Ask yourself, is it cultural that Christ rules over man? Is it cultural to God that man is head over woman? Man is head over woman because that is the way God arranged the universe.

> A man ought not to cover his head, since he is the image and glory of God; but the woman is the glory of man. For man did not come from woman, but woman from man. (1 Corinthians 11:7–8)

Does this sound like some local problem or situation? Is it really true that only in Corinth man "is the image and glory of God?" Was it only in the town of Corinth that "woman is the glory of man?" The way God made men and women lays the foundation for the command to have a "sign of authority."

Paul bases the command about a woman needing a "sign of authority" on the facts of creation. In short, the command for a covering goes all the way back to the creation of Adam and Eve. Its whole foundation rests on why woman was created.

> Neither was man created for woman, but woman for man. (1 Corinthians 11:9)

Angels

Finally Paul states that God requires women to wear a covering because of heavenly beings. The whole matter of coverings transcends earth and reaches all the way to the angels in heaven. Look closer at 1 Corinthians 11:10:

> For this reason, and *because of the angels*, the woman ought to have a sign of authority on her head. (1 Corinthians 11:10 emphasis added)

Did only the church in Corinth have angels? Doesn't your church have angels watching over it? Of course! And because of these angels, a women "ought to have a sign of authority on her head."

God made the heavens and placed angels in them. He then made the earth and created a living soul in His image. When God completed all this, He made woman, the last shining jewel to be placed on His crown called Creation. This act of creation demonstrates to God's people that women need a "sign of authority" in the church.

Nothing in 1 Corinthians 11 remotely suggests a local problem or cultural situation. Rather, the commandment has its foundation on the way God created the whole universe!

Christ's Example

Finally, Paul tells us this commandment comes straight from Jesus. There is no need for a long-winded theological debate of whether this command comes from Jesus or only Paul's opinion. The commandment for a woman to have a covering during worship comes from Jesus Himself. Paul reminds us of this fact before he begins to give us this command.

> Follow my example, as I follow the example of Christ. I praise you for remembering me in everything and for holding to the teachings, just as I passed them on to you. (1 Corinthians 11:1–2)

Paul then goes on in the following verses to explain this example of Jesus. Why do you think Paul commends them for following all the other "traditions" he has passed on to them? Because he is ready to tell them about another commandment from Jesus.

And since these people were touched by God's "grace" they are "eager" to do what is good—to obey.

> ...who gave himself for us to redeem us from all wickedness and to purify for himself a people that are his very own, eager to do what is good. (Titus 2:14)

When Satan made a frontal attack in the Garden of Eden, he went for the jugular vein. The serpent totally flip-flopped everything. Man was to be under Christ and woman under man. In order to mess everything up Satan went to the woman and got her to place herself above man and Jesus. Lucifer became the prince of this world and woman now desires to rule over man.

The struggle in the home is between who is the head, who is in control. The same spirit that the anti-Christ will revel in—control. Indeed, rebellion against God reaches its peak as women now discover they are "called of God" to preach from the pulpit.

Baldness

When angels, and God, see women in the church worshipping without a "sign of authority" they observe something very strange. They see a bunch of bald women. As Scripture puts it, "it is just as though her head were shaved." This is no minor command that can be written off as not being a salvation issue.

> And every woman who prays or prophesies with her head uncovered dishonors her head—it is just as though her head were shaved. (1 Corinthians 11:5)

Now think about it. Isn't it pretty hard to take a bald woman seriously? It makes you laugh when you think about it. So men, the next time you see a woman teaching or worshiping in church without a "sign of authority," feel free to laugh out loud. In fact men, if a woman in your church will not wear a covering while she worships, just get your clippers out and shave all her hair off. For the Bible says she should have her hair "cut off."

> If a woman does not cover her head, she should have her hair cut off; and if it is a disgrace for a woman to have her hair cut or shaved off, she should cover her head. (1 Corinthians 11:6)

So instead of snipping scriptures out of the Bible, cut the hair off the sister in church who refuses to wear a "sign of authority" on her head. Basically, women in the church have two choices—either wear a "sign of authority" or have all their hair cut off. And if it is "a disgrace for a woman to have her hair cut or shaved off, she should cover her head." If women in the church refuse to return to their proper place of authority, God will someday make their "scalps bald."

> The Lord says, "The women of Zion are haughty, walking along with outstretched necks, flirting with their eyes, tripping along with mincing steps, with ornaments jingling on their ankles. Therefore the Lord will bring sores on the heads of the women of Zion; the Lord will make their scalps bald." (Isaiah 3:16–17)

Today's Christian women dress themselves in fine clothes, jewelry, and outward acts of self-righteousness, but not with the coverings of humility that the Lord requires them to wear. They walk "along with outstretched necks" boasting and shoving to take authority. Their steps to take this rebellious authority have been a "tripping along," one small step after another to claim what is not theirs to claim. With "mincing steps" they rebel and take over positions that God never called them to. They rebel against the Most High God and the reason for their creation.

One day God will strip away such outward trappings and everyone will see clearly that most were not the nice little Christian women they claimed to be. Refusal to wear a covering reflects the rebellion in one's heart. Soon God will bring an end to all these fine looking woman leaders and preachers.

> In that day the Lord will snatch away their finery: the bangles and headbands and crescent necklaces, the earrings and bracelets and veils, the headdresses and ankle chains and sashes, the

perfume bottles and charms, the signet rings and nose rings, the fine robes and the capes and cloaks, the purses and mirrors, and the linen garments and tiaras and shawls. (Isaiah 3:18–23)

God will "snatch" away the beauty of these ministries. Note well that in keeping with our study on a "sign of authority" that soon these women preachers will experience "baldness." As Isaiah continues:

Instead of fragrance there will be a stench; instead of a sash, a rope; instead of well-dressed hair, baldness; instead of fine clothing, sackcloth; instead of beauty, branding. Your men will fall by the sword, your warriors in battle. The gates of Zion will lament and mourn; destitute, she will sit on the ground. (Isaiah 3:18–26)

Indeed, this commandment, or "sword" will kill all the men who refuse to demand that this commandment be lived. Any ministry headed by a woman, though they are rich now, will one day "sit on the ground" to "lament and mourn." Of course this commandment is not meant to put men on an ego trip. God covers all and we are all under Him. Men are not some kind of super spiritual lone rangers, they need women.

In the Lord, however, woman is not independent of man, nor is man independent of woman. For as woman came from man, so also man is born of woman. But everything comes from God. (1 Corinthians 11:11–12)

The Nature of Things

Since woman fell in the garden, holy women wear an extra "sign of authority." For you see, long hair was given to woman for everyday life. In short, God created her with a natural covering in the beginning. It was the glory God gave her.

Judge for yourselves: Is it proper for a woman to pray to God with her head uncovered? Does not the very nature of things teach you that if a man has long hair, it is a disgrace to him, but that if a woman has long hair, it is her glory? For long hair is given to her as a covering. (1 Corinthians 11:13–15)

God made women to have long hair. The "very nature of things" shows us God's intention. God gave woman this special attribute so she could reflect the glory of man through Jesus.

Watch out for those who tell you that God is not concerned with the outward appearance of a man, but only looks to the heart. After all, did He who made the soul of man not use as much care and wisdom in creating the body of man? Are our bodies not the temples of the Lord? Shall we not then decorate that temple as He directs?[11] Indeed, are not the very hairs on each of our heads numbered?[12] God is concerned about every aspect of us, this is why Scripture says to perfect holiness in both *body* and spirit." It is a total lie to say God only looks at the heart and doesn't care what we do with the body. Such doctrine merely excuses us to take authority over our bodies and do what we want. For He who put His glory in the spirits He gave us, also seeks to glorify Himself through our bodies. How we dress, comb our hair, present ourselves, whatever we do in "word or deed"[13] should reflect God's glory.

Since we have these promises, dear friends, let us purify ourselves from everything that contaminates body and spirit, perfecting holiness out of reverence for God. (2 Corinthians 7:1)

Therefore Christian women, stop sinning against God by having short hair. For as you go about your daily life, long hair tells the world that you reflect the glory of man. Long hair signifies to the world that you live in the will of God. Long hair tells the angels you agree with God's wisdom about creation. Ever notice how most women preachers or leaders have short hair?

Natural Covering

Many declare, "See, long hair is a covering." Paul simply used every argument possible to show the need for a sign of authority in church, just as we do when supporting a position. We know hair is not the covering or sign of authority because of 1 Corinthians 11:5.

> And every woman who prays or prophesies with her head un-covered dishonors her head—it is just as though her head were shaved. (1 Corinthians 11:5)

If Paul referred to natural hair he would not have said, "It is just as though her head were shaved." If hair is the covering, and these women were bald, the passage would read like this; "If her head is shaved bald and she prays, it is just as though her head were shaved bald."

Obviously, something has to be on the head for it to seem "just as *though* her head were shaved." By saying it is "as though her head were shaved," Paul made the point that in reality her head is not shaved, it only appears that way to the angels. Again, if this were not so, the passage would not make sense. Paul would be saying something like, "If she prays or prophesies bald, it is as though she is bald." People become confused because they do not realize Paul referred to two coverings. He used the natural cover-ing, the one God gave women at creation, long hair, as evidence for the need of a "sign of authority" while in church.

We know these women had hair on their heads because of verse six. Paul states that if a woman will not cover her head, she should cut her hair off. If the woman has no hair on her head, how can it be cut off?

> If a woman does not cover her head, she should have her hair cut off; and if it is a disgrace for a woman to have her hair cut or shaved off, she should cover her head. (1 Corinthians 11:6)

If hair is the covering Paul would have said, "If a woman does not have long hair, she should let it grow out because long hair is her covering." Why doesn't the scripture leave it at that? Because he discussed more than hair in this passage. If hair is the covering then why do Christian men have hair on their heads? For men are commanded:

> A man ought not to cover his head, since he is the image and glory of God. (1 Corinthians 11:7)

According to this logic, every Christian man ought to shave his head clean because hair is a covering and men must pray without a covering. If a man believes hair is the covering, then he should shave his head right now, for "a man ought not to cover his head."

Let's test the hair theory by inserting it in Scripture and see if it makes any sense to you. Read the Scripture according to the logic of hair being the covering. "Every man who prays or prophesies with his HAIR ON HIS HEAD dishonors his head. And every woman who prays or prophesies WITHOUT HAIR dishonors her head—it is just as though her head were shaved. If a woman does not HAVE LONG HAIR, she should have her hair cut off; and if it is a disgrace for a woman to have her hair cut or shaved off, she should HAVE HER HAIR CUT OFF." (1 Corinthians 11:4–6 other words added)

Token of Authority

Let us remember that we are talking about a "sign of authority." Something out of the ordinary that demonstrates to all, even angels, that women remain in submission to men. Young's Literal Greek text puts it this way.

> Because of this the woman ought to have a token of authority upon the head, because of the messengers. (1 Corinthians 11:10)

The word token is a perfect definition for this passage. Styish hats that women used to wear in the church as a "sign of authority" were compromise. In an attempt to wear something that looked like obedience to God, yet didn't require humility, they started wearing hats. A token of authority must be something specifically set aside for that purpose. Just as we are to be holy, set aside for

God, so too there needs to be a token, something set aside for the head that reflects a sign of authority.

token (t1/2"k?n) n. 1. Something serving as an indication, a proof, or an expression of something else; a sign. 2. Something that signifies or evidences authority, validity, or identity.

The "sign of authority" is "proof, or an expression," of what resides in the heart and soul. Unbelieving women in the world may have long hair, but for them it is a symbol of sensuality and vanity, not submission. For this reason God requires a second covering during worship. Remember what we saw earlier? When God made man and woman their natural hair length was a symbol of their inward spirituality and submission to His design.

When we fell so did those symbols and our acceptance of His plan. When a woman returns to the Lord she regains her God-given spiritual status. This new covering symbolizes her agreement with God in this matter. The sign of authority depicts a beautiful picture of the blood of Jesus that covers over our sins and the Holy Spirit's anointing oil that blesses the woman of grace.

No Other Practice

Churches often use the next passage to discount everything Paul just wrote about coverings.

If anyone wants to be contentious about this, we have no other practice—nor do the churches of God. (1 Corinthians 11:16)

Mockers of God often misinterpret this passage to mean that the first churches did not practice wearing a "sign of authority." Why would Paul write all he wrote about the need for a covering and then say, "Gee fellas, never mind we don't really practice this?"

Paul stated that whether in Rome, Athens, Spain, or Israel, in all the "churches of God" all the women wore coverings. Consider again that all these towns had different cultures and worldly traditions, yet Paul told the Corinthians that "we have no other practice" than that of coverings. Next time you are reading a news report from missionaries overseas notice how many photographs show women wearing coverings. In fact, many women visiting overseas from America are forced to wear a covering. Thankfully the American style of delusion hasn't infiltrated everywhere yet. All those churches conducted worship in the "fitting way" God had intended.

> But everything should be done in a fitting and orderly way. (1 Corinthians 14:40)

"But everything," that is, everything, should be done in a way that God set down. The Word says our God is a God of order. Therefore there is a proper procedure for women to "pray or prophecy" while in church or in a group.

The sign of authority permits a women to "pray or prophesy" in church. Prophecy of course is not preaching and the praying is done only under the watchful eye of the men in church. When a women's "head" is "uncovered" it is improper "for a woman to pray to God" in the church. You will need a good conscience and a sincere faith to be able to "judge for yourself."[14]

> Judge for yourselves: Is it proper for a woman to pray to God with her head uncovered? (1 Corinthians 11:13)

When a woman worships at church or even a home Bible study, she should wear her covering, or sign of authority, on her head. During this time, since men are in leadership, overseeing, and in positions of responsibility, the covering should remain. In this way she will reflect the heart of God and declare to men on earth and the angels in the heavens that she understands how to glorify God.

Reflecting God's Glory

The covering does not cover the face, for that would cloud from view the glory of Christ. A covering on the head shows that a woman acknowledges that man is above her. She has someone above her in addition to God, for a woman has two above her, God and man, therefore she has two coverings. Long hair symbolizes woman's submission to man and a covering her submission to God. She does not cover her face because we have a greater covenant than the one Moses received. We each, with open faces, reflect the glory of the Lord.

And we, who with unveiled faces all reflect the Lord's glory, are being transformed into his likeness with ever-increasing glory, which comes from the Lord, who is the Spirit. (2 Corinthians 3:18)

Unlike Moses whose glory faded, women continue to grow in God's glory and plan. Therefore, let everyone see the glory coming from her face. We are not to be like Moses . . .

We are not like Moses, who would put a veil over his face to keep the Israelites from gazing at it while the radiance was fading away. (2 Corinthians 3:13)

Man does not wear a covering because only God is above him. Therefore little hats, Yarmulkes, that the Messianic churches wear, are sin and only produce pride. For God is clear that a man is not to worship with any covering on his head. Indeed, when they wear the Yarmulke they dishonor God.

Every man who prays or prophesies with his head covered dishonors his head. (1 Corinthians 11:4)

A man ought not to cover his head, since he is the image and glory of God; but the woman is the glory of man. (1 Corinthians 11:7)

Ignoring This Command

Paul begins his instructions about proper worship in 1 Corinthians 11 and ends it in 1 Corinthians 14. Throughout this section of Corinthians, Paul lays out the traditions for coverings, the Lord's Supper, spiritual gifts, unity, love, silence in church, and the proper use of tongues and prophecy. As Paul closes his instructions about the matters of conduct in the church, he writes by the authority of the Holy Spirit the following command.

> For God is not a God of disorder but of peace. As in all the congregations of the saints, women should remain silent in the churches. They are not allowed to speak, but must be in submission, as the Law says. If they want to inquire about something, they should ask their own husbands at home; for it is disgraceful for a woman to speak in the church. Did the word of God originate with you? Or are you the only people it has reached? If anybody thinks he is a prophet or spiritually gifted, let him acknowledge that what I am writing to you is the Lord's command. If he ignores this, he himself will be ignored. (1 Corinthians 14:33–38)

Paul spoke sharply and sarcastically about this matter because he knew that in our sinful nature we would not readily obey this command. The cross always cuts across our flesh. Paul states that if anyone ignores these issues of such importance then they must be "ignored."

Because this is the Lord's command, Paul told us to "ignore" anyone who does not demand that this be lived out. That's right, no matter how spiritual you think your pastor is, (verse: 37) or how much he knows about the Word of God, (verse: 36) if there is no demand to obey this commandment, he must be totally ignored. Until he repents and comes to the knowledge of this you can't listen to his sermons, eat with him at the church social, or even help mow the church lawn. You can't even answer the phone when the pastor calls until he says that the church will obey this from the heart by the power of the Holy Spirit. The reason is simple. There is more power and spirituality in this practice than first meets the eye. This command is important and powerful to God—its truth can be seen in the way God designed and arranged the universe.

Women, can the angels tell when you sit in church that you agree with God's plan of submission? Can they see your godliness or do they see you as you really are, a bald woman? Does your beauty come from a "quiet spirit?" Are you in agreement that when you go to church you must be "silent" and let men run the show? Do you only speak up with the permission of the leaders and with a token sign that shows you have a sign of authority and their permission to speak?

The False Church

Of course the false church in the last days hotly rejects and opposes such teaching. Indeed a very large and massive false Christian church will soon persecute the remnant. Women pastors and men rejecting their God-given manhood will start and maintain this false church. God will allow this false doctrine, that women can teach and have authority over a man to be confirmed with blessings, prophecies, dreams, visions, and wisdom. It is the Powerful Delusion, the insanity of pride, boasting, and self-fulfillment glorified, blessed, and flourished. It is rebellion against God's perfect plan and a full rejection of the cross of Christ. All because men were the first to reject the message of humility many, many years ago.

We can look back over the years to see the tree starting to dry up. Go back 60 years and there was still a contrast in the message between the world and the church. Women knew their proper place in the home and church. In the 1980s the church crossed over to the world and more women went to work. In the 1990s the church blessed the love of the world and encouraged women to enter the pulpits. In the 2000s we can only imagine how the love of the world may usher in the anti-Christ. Pray that you escape all that is about to happen and that you will be able to "stand before the Son of Man."

> Be always on the watch, and pray that you may be able to escape all that is about to happen, and that you may be able to stand before the Son of Man." (Luke 21:36)

Chapter 6

MONEY MADNESS

...and in every sort of evil that deceives those who are perishing. They perish because they refused to love the truth and so be saved. (2 Thessalonians 2:10)

"Every sort of evil" has been unleashed in the church, but the sin of loving money towers over all sin. Satan uses money to influence, move, and motivate men to do all manner of evil. Satan will unite the world against true Christians through money. Money controls man and Satan will use its power. All through history, Satan has enjoyed corrupting the church with money. Satan greatly desires for men to have money in its "proper perspective." Best-selling books in Christian bookstores expound on using money "wisely," or with a "proper perspective." However, they know nothing of the offensive cross and the crucified life. Such books are worse than neutral good advice, they get in the way of the will of God. Were one to remove religious quotes from these materials, it would read just like any other worldly investment book. The messages contain common sense advice on how to use money in the world, not the cross that makes a man poor.[1] The writers never mention a Jesus that demands we "give up everything."

In the same way, any of you who does not give up everything he has cannot be my disciple. (Luke 14:33)

"Go sell everything you have" and come follow Him is not declared.[2]

Jesus answered, "If you want to be perfect, go, sell your possessions and give to the poor, and you will have treasure in heaven. Then come, follow me." (Matthew 19:21)

If the books contained or understood in the smallest degree the "message of the cross" they would not be bestsellers. If we are to be like Jesus, then we must follow in His footsteps. Footsteps that lead to personal poverty because we make others rich.

For you know the grace of our Lord Jesus Christ, that though he was rich, yet for your sakes he became poor, so that you through his poverty might become rich. (2 Corinthians 8:9)

Paul, a mighty example of the power of the cross knew this reality in his life. He would have found no use for the money advice that fills the church and bookstores today. Indeed, not only does his life still rebuke such things, but he would have judged them if he were alive today.

sorrowful, yet always rejoicing; poor, yet making many rich; having nothing, and yet possessing everything. (2 Corinthians 6:10)

No greater evil do we see in the church than the love of money. The insanity effects even those who think they have money in its "proper perspective." Jesus has only one perspective on money. He who does not "hate" and "despise" money, loves it. Period. There is no middle ground. Men will often quote 1 Timothy 6:10 "For the love of money is a root of all kinds of evil." They will declare with a cool conscience they don't "love money." In fact, if anyone mentions that Jesus said we must "hate" and "despise" money the automatic response is to declare, "That is right. It is the love of money that is wrong, but not money itself." But how does a man know if he really doesn't love money? The answer, as with everything, is to look at Jesus and the cross He carried. Jesus told us how we could know if we love money or not. If we do not "hate" and "despise" money, we love it.

> "No servant can serve two masters. Either he will hate the one and love the other, or he will be devoted to the one and despise the other. You cannot serve both God and Money." (Luke 16:13)

We can only not love money by obeying Jesus. By the power of the Holy Spirit, through the cross, we must come to "hate" and "despise" money. If we do not have these attitudes, we cannot serve God. This book will not take the time to explain how to hate money, but will focus on how the Powerful Delusion blesses greed. For the moment let us understand that desiring more than "food and clothing" constitutes greed in God's sight.[3] After all, greed is the desire for more than what we have, and God has told us to be "content" with "food and clothing." Any desire for something beyond that is greed. Being worried and concerned beyond daily bread and clothing is sin before the Lord.[4]

Lot's Wife

Every person must remember "Lot's wife," who simply turned her head to see if the world she knew would be utterly destroyed. She looked back because she missed something more important to her than fleeing the wrath of God. For you it may be a picture of the family, a friend, a dress, or a keepsake. There must arise a deep and very serious rejection of the world if we want to escape the wrath to come. We are to be a people so crucified to the world that we will not "go back for anything." If we do not lose our life now, we will lose it for eternal life. So let us conclude at the outset that desiring, liking, or wanting even one thing is greed. Think of Satan's trap. He steam rolls the economy, getting everyone used to money and fun, adds in a measure of spirituality, even using Scripture to bless the materialism, then brings it all crashing down.

Satan addicts us to our sin and then in order to feed the addiction, we must come to him.

> On that day no one who is on the roof of his house, with his goods inside, should go down to get them. Likewise, no one in the field should go back for anything. Remember Lot's wife! Whoever tries to keep his life will lose it, and whoever loses his life will preserve it. (Luke 17:31–33)

Despising Money

Now don't fall for the Exaggeration Justification trap. We always think there are individuals more greedy and vile than ourselves. To look at someone else for a justification that you don't love money will prove to be a very costly mistake. It will cost you your soul. In reality, money controls us more than we want to admit. For who can resist a good sale? Who doesn't say, "Praise God, I got this bargain." We rejoice as if God needed a bargain in order to help His people get through another day. How easily saving 15% motivates us to sign up early for a seminar. From radio shows that give away free items, to coupons and contests, we let money fulfill and motivate us far too easily. Therefore, Jesus said we must not only "hate," but also "despise" money. It is interesting to note that Jesus said you only have to "hate" your life, father, mother, wife, children, brothers, sisters but when it comes to money you have to also "despise" money.[5]

Listen to the warning. Unless you willingly allow God to teach you how to "hate" and "despise" money, you leave yourself wide open to the insanity in the church. Indeed, God will see to it, as we have already seen, that you will take the mark of the beast. For only those who know how to despise the dollar on a daily basis will have the grace, and thus the power, to refuse the mark of the beast.

We live in a time when the Pharisees and religious church goers "sneer" at any mention of this money issue. Greed and the love of money have been so loudly preached that many give into this without even realizing it. They feel no pain in the conscience as they keep money in its proper perspective.

The Pharisees, who loved money, heard all this and were sneering at Jesus. He said to them, "You are the ones who justify yourselves in the eyes of men, but God knows your hearts. What is highly valued among men is detestable in God's sight. (Luke 16:14–15)

Before we move on, notice how God views money. Jesus declares it is, "detestable in God's sight." It is a vile, wicked thing that only fallen, evil man could invent. Money never entered God's mind or heart. Money is, in and of itself, a wicked thing. Because men "highly value" money, God permits the Powerful Delusion to bless it. Again as we take a look at the worst of the money blessers, keep in mind and heart that anyone who does not hate money, loves it.

Turn back and examine your own heart first, for if we cannot be found "trustworthy" in hating and despising "worldly wealth" why would Jesus ever give us "true riches?" No wonder God cannot give the church true riches of self-discipline and His holiness— He cannot trust us to hate and dispise money. Since we have not been "trustworthy" to do this, we are left to our own devices, gimmicks and wisdom.

So if you have not been trustworthy in handling worldly wealth, who will trust you with true riches? (Luke 16:11)

The arrogance of prosperity churches is utterly amazing. They love money and refuse to hate it, and still think God pours out miracles and spiritual gifts. God does not give "true riches," grace, love, mercy, or fellowship to those who refuse to despise money.

Prosperity teachers, those who teach that God wants to bless His people with worldly goods, lead the Powerful Delusion and are the most deluded and insane. They far surpass the Pharisees of Jesus' time that could "justify" themselves in the eyes of men, because prosperity teachers use the words of Jesus to bless their covetousness. They are experts in greed, knowing how to make it look holy and normal. The yeast Jesus warned us about spreads through the whole batch of dough. Prosperity teachers are experts in making the outside of the cup look good while they remain full of greed. They know how to mix their love of money with teachings about giving to the poor. They use noble causes to justify their greed. They declare in magazines that they are kings but inside are full of "greed" and "self-indulgence."

> Woe to you, teachers of the law and Pharisees, you hypocrites! You clean the outside of the cup and dish, but inside they are full of greed and self-indulgence. (Matthew 23:25)

In Balaam's Footsteps

These Pharisees are the priests helping to prepare a people and the world for the anti-Christ. What a scheme of Satan! He fills the church with false prosperity prophets while turning up the economy, getting us used to the pleasure of a detestable thing, only to bring it all down upon our heads later. The insanity of the prosperity teachers infiltrates the conservative church even while it condemns the teaching. The conservatives feel safe, but do not despise the dollar themselves. Although they stand firm against the prosperity teachers by human logic, they will not find the grace to resist the anti-Christ.[6]

When the situation arises where no one can buy or sell without Satan's approval, a great falling away will happen as Jesus predicted. People will not have the grace to resist since they fed the flesh for too long. Like the foolish virgins, they will only have enough oil to get them through one day, with no extra for the dark days of the Lord.[7] Of course the prosperity people will be devastated and unable to resist the anti-Christ because denying self is a totally foreign concept to them. Only those on the very "straight way" of hating and despising the dollar by the power of the Holy Spirit will not "wander[ed] off to follow the way of Balaam."

> They have left the straight way and wandered off to follow the way of Balaam son of Beor, who loved the wages of wickedness. (2 Peter 2:15)

Balaam, because he did not hate and despise money, loved it. He wanted God to allow him to be blessed with riches and prosperity in this world. Like Balaam, prosperity teachers have become "experts in greed." They know just how to preach a sermon in such a way as to make it sound logical, holy, and righteous to be greedy. They commit adultery against the Lord and are loaded down with all kinds of sin. They preach and gain large followings by seducing those "unstable" in the Lord. For only those "unstable" in the church follow the teachings of the prosperity teachers and their doctrine. Like an adulterer they have "eyes full" looking for new converts to seduce.

> With eyes full of adultery, they never stop sinning; they seduce the unstable; they are experts in greed—an accursed brood! (2 Peter 2:14)

Springs Without Water

The prosperity teachers are "an accursed brood," and there is indeed a whole "brood" of them. This is hard for most people to accept. Since the average Christian has not allowed God to teach them how to "hate" and "despise" money, they find it hard to pronounce judgment against these teachers, for to condemn them is to judge themselves. Nevertheless they are "an accursed brood" for whom the "blackest" of "darkness" in hell is "reserved."

> These men are springs without water and mists driven by a storm. Blackest darkness is reserved for them. (2 Peter 2:17)

These teachers look like they have the river of life, but are "springs without water." They appear strong in the Lord, so confident in their faith, but are "mists driven by a storm." Not only can you gain nothing from them, but to follow any of their teachings is to share a corner of blackest darkness with them. For to love the flesh, money, and self in the name of the Lord is a worse crime then being an atheist and living for money. Better to be honest and live for self, than use the name of the Lord to justify sin.

Just listen to the prosperity teachings and preachings. They boast of God's power and stomping on the devil. They appeal to man's flesh in order to win converts to Jesus. After all, who doesn't in their flesh want to be rich, disease free, and victorious in a worldly way at all times. They appeal "to the lustful desires of sinful human nature" to win folks over. Who wouldn't want to be out of debt, have a financial breakthrough, retire early, and live a comfortable life in this world?

Have you ever noticed, however, their style of preaching? They "mouth empty, boastful words," laying claim to heaven and earth while they mock Satan, shouting and laughing at him. They boast and ensnare those who are just starting to come to God.

> For they mouth empty, boastful words and, by appealing to the lustful desires of sinful human nature, they entice people who are just escaping from those who live in error. (2 Peter 2:18)

Good Beginnings

This chapter looks at prosperity teachers, the worst of the lot, but many churches are growing in the Powerful Delusion concerning money. The idea that the church needs to show the world it can have fun and be blessed like the world has invaded multitudes of groups. Churches that would fully reject the prosperity teachers remain just as insane, but in a quieter way. For like the prosperity leaders, they "promise" others "freedom" in Jesus, but do not understand in the least what the crucified life is all about. They are also "mastered" by the self that lives in them even as they go about their religious work.

> They promise them freedom, while they themselves are slaves of depravity—for a man is a slave to whatever has mastered him. (2 Peter 2:19)

Many of these prosperity teachers, and those who do not "hate" and "despise" money, started out following Jesus. But when the road became too narrow and too long they turned their backs on God one inch at a time.

As a very young Christian, just starting to carry my cross, I heard a sermon preached on radio by one of the granddaddies of the prosperity movement. I couldn't believe what I heard. It was exact and powerful as he preached about the crucified life and the power of hating one's life for Jesus. I thought to myself, *How can this be? How can he understand the cross and still preach such a terrible lie?*

I listened on until the sermon finished and then the announcement came that made everything clear. The announcer stated, "That was a very old sermon done many years ago." The comment sent terror into my heart, for I knew that if God did not crucify the greed in me, one day I could be like him, having known the truth, but then finding the road too hard and turning back to the world. Peter describes such men.

> If they have escaped the corruption of the world by knowing our Lord and Savior Jesus Christ and are again entangled in it and overcome, they are worse off at the end than they were at the beginning. It would have been better for them not to have known the way of righteousness, than to have known it and then to turn their backs on the sacred command that was passed on to them. Of them the proverbs are true: "A dog returns to its vomit," and, "A sow that is washed goes back to her wallowing in the mud." (2 Peter 2:20–22)

As men turn cold toward Jesus in the last days, instead of just returning to the world, they will "wallow" in the mud of the world while singing, "Jesus we love you." They will eat the "vomit" of money, while they chew on God's Word, the most detestable mixture for a man to eat. Is it any wonder that God reserves such heavy judgment for them? As Peter declares, "it would have been better for them not to have known the way of righteousness." Better to die a God hating atheist than to die a prosperity teacher or believer who has money in its proper perspective. Hell is bad enough, but the blackest darkness in hell cannot be comprehended by the human mind. If you want to view how God views prosperity teachers, then go watch a dog eat vomit.

Church Business

The church wallows in the mud like the prosperity teacher, selling everything. We are insane, wanting to promote our ministry, our name, or our cause. The church is loaded down with moneychangers. It has gotten so bad that even the world wants to tax the churches, and rightly so. The church has become more like a business than a sanctuary. The church should be known as a "house of prayer" and a sanctuary from the world. Get rid of the business in your church and get on with the business of the gospel. When someone goes to church it should be a place of rest from the world. Yet the church today boasts that it is like the mall, with coffee shops and books stores in the main lobby. Sales, coupons, savings accounts, IRAs, and early registrations motivate Christians just as they do the world. The church believes that the inheritance mentioned in Proverbs 13:22 refers to money. They do not understand that true riches are not money, or how God often uses earthly things to demonstrate a deeper truth.[8] The church points to David's riches, not his planned poverty, purpose, and sufferings for God.[9] They don't show by their lives or their words that they understand why David was given wealth.

> Then King David said to the whole assembly: "My son Solomon, the one whom God has chosen, is young and inexperienced. The task is great, because this palatial structure is not for man but for the Lord God. With all my resources I have provided for the temple of my God—gold for the gold work, silver for the silver, bronze for the bronze, iron for the iron and wood for the wood, as well as onyx for the settings, turquoise, stones of various colors, and all kinds of fine stone and marble—all of these in large quantities. Besides, in my devotion to the temple of my God I now give my personal treasures of gold and silver for the temple of my God, over and above everything I have provided

for this holy temple: three thousand talents of gold (gold of Ophir) and seven thousand talents of refined silver, for the overlaying of the walls of the buildings, for the gold work and the silver work, and for all the work to be done by the craftsmen. Now, who is willing to consecrate himself today to the Lord?" (1 Chronicles 29:1–5)

David, before he died, gave his "personal treasures of gold and silver for the temple of my God, over and above everything [he] had provided for this holy temple." Those who have money handled can't hold a candle to the heart of David—a man whose heart burned only for the temple of the Lord, who counted nothing he owned as personal gain. David not only spoke words of such devotion and truth, but his life matched it also. Unless we who have the fullness of the Truth in the message of the cross surpass this by hating and despising money, we live a lie.

Covering Costs

Indeed everyone wants to cover their costs as they sell their wares, products, and sermon tapes in the church. For over twenty years our church never charged, hinted, or begged for money. Everything has been given away free, because that is the way of the cross and according to Jesus' command. Jesus said, "freely give."

> Heal the sick, raise the dead, cleanse those who have leprosy, drive out demons. Freely you have received, freely give. (Matthew 10:8)

How pathetic that you even have to buy this book. For neither the church, nor individual Christians know how to "hate" and "despise" money any more. Few give without being promised something in return and this puts undue pressure on churches and ministries to charge for items.

On the other hand, most ministries have forgotten that Jesus overturns tables when we sell things in His name. In fact, it was the only time Jesus displayed full-blown anger. The insanity of the

Powerful Delusion has so watered us down that few people have any anger about the situation concerning money in the church. The insanity has increased so much, that ministries use Christian celebrities to get people to help feed the poor overseas! There needs to be some whip snapping and table turning in almost every ministry. No wonder the zeal for purity in God's house is at an all-time low. We are not "consume[d]" with "zeal" for God's "house" and so with each passing day the church looks more and more like a marketplace.

> So he made a whip out of cords, and drove all from the temple area, both sheep and cattle; he scattered the coins of the money changers and overturned their tables. To those who sold doves he said, "Get these out of here! How dare you turn my Father's house into a market!" His disciples remembered that it is written: "Zeal for your house will consume me." (John 2:15–17)

Forced to Sell

The love of most grows cold, as Jesus said it would in the last days, and the zeal for God's house dies. Churches, ministries, and Christians trade, sell, barter, and get their fair share without even a hint of shame. We have grown so used to comfortable giving where we check a box and receive something in return for our donation that we feel no shame. Ministries are forced to sell items because the giving by others is not from a selfless heart.

People will often ask how our church can give away so many things for free. They are literally astonished by all that God does. They think we have some magic gimmick. The answer of course is good old fashion sacrifice and faith. Nothing loud or worth promoting, just simple cross carrying, rich faith in God.

Ministries have been forced to beg for supplies because of the heart of the average Christian. Those who smugly whine about the sin of selling sermon tapes and goods are the very last to give for what they take from the church. A double-edged sword must be used when discussing true repentance. This insanity has so grown that many fine organizations that help suffering Christians must put a catalog in the center of their news magazine. Do we really need a coffee cup about suffering Christians? Or a music CD to support our persecuted brothers and sisters? No longer can groups just appeal to the cross and to the Holy Spirit to motivate people to respond to a need. We live in desperate times when the very "foundations are being destroyed" in the church so what is a ministry to do?

> When the foundations are being destroyed, what can the righteous do? (Psalms 11:3)

Silver and Gold

No longer is poverty in the Lord held up as a goal. No longer are the poor in the church looked to for spiritual wisdom. The church insults the poor and places the rich and successful in positions of authority and ministry.

> Listen, my dear brothers: Has not God chosen those who are poor in the eyes of the world to be rich in faith and to inherit the kingdom he promised those who love him? (James 2:5)

Let us listen again to the words of God when He tells us He has "chosen those who are poor in the eyes of the world to be rich in faith." The rich, successful, and powerful ministries do not give us the understanding of real faith. Instead, let us look to the poor in the Body who can say, "Silver and gold I do not have."

> Then Peter said, "Silver or gold I do not have, but what I have I give you. In the name of Jesus Christ of Nazareth, walk." (Acts 3:6)

Is it not amazing how all these modern day miracle worship sermons are rich in gold and silver? It is amazing how they have become kings and gods when Peter who walked with the Lord on earth was still so poor. Or how Paul was "poor, yet making many rich."[10] Paul rebuked the Corinthians for this superior attitude of thinking they are "kings."

Already you have all you want! Already you have become rich! You have become kings—and that without us! How I wish that you really had become kings so that we might be kings with you! (1 Corinthians 4:8)

The truth is, we are not kings, but bondservants who might become kings in the Lord if we remain faithful unto death. Right now no one is a king in the Lord. We are still creatures of the fall and only those who remain faithful will be rewarded. For now, all who live in the world, whether Christian or non-Christian, still have weeds in their gardens, they still have to work for a living, they get sick, and women still have great pain in childbirth. The fact is, God often uses our sufferings to preach the gospel and even permits an "illness" so that we might be given a chance to share Jesus.[11] Indeed, for a true Christian, suffering only increases when they follow Jesus because all of hell rages against them.

A Clear Distinction

You do not have to be a spiritual giant to see who rewards these miracle workers of today. God permits Satan to reward them so men will follow a lie. Only those who understand money's true perspective, who have the heart of God in the matter will see through these vile men. The question is, can you see through yourself? Are you repulsed by men who beg, ask, plead, urge, and motivate others to give by offering items for them to buy? Do you demand that your church no longer have a store or business in its building? Are you worn out with all the borrowing and lending among brothers and sisters that you see going on in the church?

I don't know about you, but I cannot wait for the anti-Christ to come on the world stage. For then there will be no gray area. God will set up a situation where there will be only two camps. You will not have the luxury of saying someone loves God, or that they have good fruit because it will be revealed one way or another. There will only be those who have money and love it and those who have no money and despise it.

Soon God will set the price for a day's bread. It will take a whole day of labor just to buy a "quart of wheat." It will be a welcomed release from the hypocrisy one must endure today. For either a man will have the mark of the beast, or he will not.

> Then I heard what sounded like a voice among the four living creatures, saying, "A quart of wheat for a day's wages, and three quarts of barley for a day's wages, and do not damage the oil and the wine!" (Revelation 6:6)

Of course the "oil and the wine" of the Holy Spirit will not be damaged. Those who know God will be given power to endure those days and to rejoice at their coming. They will rejoice over the distinction between those who love money and those who hate it.[12] For either you will take the mark of the beast so that you can make money or you will be deprived of *all* money.

> He also forced everyone, small and great, rich and poor, free and slave, to receive a mark on his right hand or on his forehead, so that no one could buy or sell unless he had the mark, which is the name of the beast or the number of his name. (Revelation 13:16–17)

This hour of decision will be "forced" on the whole world. Gone will be every ministry work, every calling, all fun and food; except for those willing to take the mark. Slowly and not so slowly one can see the love for Jesus turning cold as the vast majority of the "church" embraces the love of money.

No Shame

So many, cold in the Lord concerning money, think that this coolness toward God is normal and of course it is easy to look hot when everyone around is cold. Like the church in the Old Testament, we no longer blush about sin. "Are they ashamed of their loathsome conduct?" Jeremiah asks even as he answers the question. The same is true today, people just will "not listen" and take warning about the Powerful Delusion coming on the scene.

> Are they ashamed of their loathsome conduct? No, they have no shame at all; they do not even know how to blush. So they will fall among the fallen; they will be brought down when I punish them," says the Lord. This is what the Lord says: "Stand at the crossroads and look; ask for the ancient paths, ask where the good way is, and walk in it, and you will find rest for your souls. But you said, 'We will not walk in it.' I appointed watchmen over you and said, 'Listen to the sound of the trumpet!' But you said, 'We will not listen.'" (Jeremiah 6:15–17)

Let us obey verse 16, stand at the "crossroads and look" for the "ancient paths" that are "good." Look to the New Testament church for an example. After their very lives had been "shaken" by the Holy Spirit what fruit was produced? Lives freed from the love of money and things. They had hearts that despised money with great zeal. Without rules, regulations or the church leadership taking everyone's property, they willingly let the Holy Spirit work the "hating" and "despising" of money.

> After they prayed, the place where they were meeting was shaken. And they were all filled with the Holy Spirit and spoke the word of God boldly. All the believers were one in heart and mind. No one claimed that any of his possessions was his own, but they shared everything they had. With great power the apostles continued to testify to the resurrection of the Lord Jesus, and much grace was upon them all. (Acts 4:31–33)

New Joy

Until the church allows the Holy Spirit to put money and things in God's proper perspective—as detestable—the church will never have true unity. No wonder the first church preached with true power and much "grace was upon them all." Self was crucified and set free from money.

Hating and despising money is one of the greatest freedoms a person can experience. Each day you can find a new freedom and a new joy to experience as you live this out. Even as a church our joy grows as we have "all things in common," never "claiming" that anything belongs to ourselves. And all of this happens without rules, regulations, or programs, but by the simple working of the Holy Spirit through the cross.

This joy in the Lord, this Festival, causes true Christians to not want fellowship with anyone who claims to be a Christian, but is greedy, as defined by Jesus. After all how can those who love money enjoy fellowship with those who hate it? And how can those who despise the dollar find a common point of reference with those who tolerate money? Indeed, they cannot get along and those who hate and despise money will be driven to not associate with them. When hearts beat the same, sweet fellowship follows in the Lord. If you claim to be a Christian, get on with letting the Lord show you how to hate and despise money. If you refuse to allow God to work this, don't expect to eat lunch with those who do.

> But now I am writing you that you must not associate with anyone who calls himself a brother but is sexually immoral or greedy, an idolater or a slanderer, a drunkard or a swindler. *With such a man do not even eat.* (1 Corinthians 5:11 emphasis added)

Holy Judgement

Let there arise a spirit of holy judgment in the church in these the last days. Let it start first with a resounding denunciation of prosperity teachers. Not talk, debate, or reasoning, but a total rebuke that denounces this teaching, its preachers and followers. Right now hardly a whimper can be heard. Oh, we debate, we talk, we discuss, we reason, but we do not denounce. We are not even as bold as Balaam's donkey who "rebuked" his master. A donkey that stood its ground, crushed his master's leg, and rebuked him in the clearest of terms.

Can't we as a church at least come up to the level of Balaam's donkey? Where is the indignation, the fire of excommunication?

Where is the holy anger and lives that match those rebukes? Like the apostles we remain too enthralled with our ministries, projects, and church buildings to see the widows around us put into the temple treasury everything they have to live on.

> Calling his disciples to him, Jesus said, "I tell you the truth, this poor widow has put more into the treasury than all the others. They all gave out of their wealth; but she, out of her poverty, put in everything—all she had to live on." (Mark 12:43–44)

We don't see the widow's copper coins because we want the approval of those powerful in the church. We stand too enthralled with the "magnificent" mega churches to give any attention to what Jesus says about the "poor widow." Oh that those who love God would wake up. Better to fellowship with a humble poor widow than to even notice a magnificent ministry. Like the disciples we cannot see what Jesus sees, viewing money as He does, because we love the impressive ministries in our towns.

> As he was leaving the temple, one of his disciples said to him, "Look, Teacher! What massive stones! What magnificent buildings!" (Mark 13:1)

True Revival

We say to Jesus, "Look, Teacher!" and go on to talk about our churches, projects, and "magnificent" ministries. We are such fools. Let us pray that we would no longer be fools. Pray that true revival would happen in the land where all who profess to give all to God, but hold back some for themselves would be struck dead by the Holy Spirit. Let us pray for a movement of the Holy Spirit that would strike and kill those who outwardly look like they give all to God, but inside privately hold back for themselves. Little wonder we never hear prayers for revival like this, for if God really moved His Spirit like this again, the vast majority of churches would be nothing but ruins piled high with dead bodies. For like Ananias, many keep some for themselves as they profess to give all. So many people claim to give all to God, but still live for self. May God strike them dead. Indeed, He will, but for now the Powerful Delusion weeds out false Christians.

> Then Peter said, "Ananias, how is it that Satan has so filled your heart that you have lied to the Holy Spirit and have kept for yourself some of the money you received for the land? Didn't it belong to you before it was sold? And after it was sold, wasn't the money at your disposal? What made you think of doing such a thing? You have not lied to men but to God." When Ananias heard this, he fell down and died. And great fear seized all who heard what had happened. Then the young men came forward, wrapped up his body, and carried him out and buried him. About three hours later his wife came in, not knowing what had happened. (Acts 5:3–7)

Let all who are "young men" in the Lord carry the bodies out and bury them. Let them consider with much seriousness what it really means to call oneself a "Christian." Twice in Acts 5 God records that young men came forward and carried out the bodies of Ananias and his wife. Now is the time to repent. To ask the Holy Spirit to teach you how to pick up a cross that will instruct you how to view money as God does. Walk in the footsteps of these young men and think what they thought as they marched out of the city to bury those struck by the Lord.

We fast approach the time of the anti-Christ, when all that will be required, in order to have money, is to take a small mark. Anyone who does not take this mark will not be able to buy, sell, or have fun. Do not fool yourself, unless you can die to money now, God will see to it you take the mark of the beast. Unless you become sane in Jesus, you will embrace the mark of the beast as a blessing from God. If we can't say "no" to the influences of coupons in our buying and selling, how will we ever stand against the anti-Christ? Is it little wonder our gospel calls get cheaper and cheaper as everyone looks for a discount! It's a Powerful Delusion indeed.

Chapter 7

MIRACLE MADNESS

A wicked and adulterous generation looks for a miraculous sign, but none will be given it except the sign of Jonah." Jesus then left them and went away. (Matthew 16:4)

Miracle madness has invaded the church. Because the church is loaded down with sin and self, the unholy desire for miracles abounds. Miracles have become the proof of being blessed in God. Men mock prayers in the Bible and promises in Scriptures, and they study books to obtain blessings and miracles. Since men reject the offensive message of the cross, the only thing that seems to be understood is the "sign of Jonah," that Jesus died because of our sins. But such a sign is not enough to save a man.

Today people think miracles are proof of God's presence. Divine appointments create specific blessings and situations providing proof that God is with them. This deadly trap always leaves us with more and more dissatisfaction. For like a drug addict, greater miracles are needed to give people the high that they seek from God.

No wonder that the anti-Christ will achieve his worship by the use of a great miracle. For mankind will have become bored with all our small personal miracles and will hunger for something much greater. Soon all the miracle loving worshipers of Jesus will be "astonished" at a great miracle, and because they were not dead to self, will follow the beast.

> One of the heads of the beast seemed to have had a fatal wound, but the fatal wound had been healed. The whole world was astonished and followed the beast. (Revelation 13:3)

Do Not Rejoice

Only a return to the message of the cross that causes one to "suffer" in order to deal with sin will save us.[1] Just look at the attitude of Jesus as He headed to Jerusalem to die on the cross. Consider that Jesus denounced most of the cities in which He performed miracles. Jesus felt frustrated that the people would not respond to the truth but loved His miracles instead.

> Then Jesus began to denounce the cities in which most of his miracles had been performed, because they did not repent. (Matthew 11:20)

Jesus commanded us not to rejoice in the ability to do powerful miracles in His name. Yet today the church shouts, broadcasts, boasts, and uses such things to gain a larger and larger following.

> However, do not rejoice that the spirits submit to you, but rejoice that your names are written in heaven. (Luke 10:20)

Jesus often sent others away before doing miracles. He always kept the people and miraculous events low key. Now, of course, with insanity the norm everyone talks about their miraculous filled lives.

> When he arrived at the house of Jairus, he did not let anyone go in with him except Peter, John and James, and the child's father and mother. (Luke 8:51)

Jesus often told people not to tell anyone about his miracles, but to go live a quiet, contemplative, holy life as a good witness to others.

"See that you don't tell this to anyone. But go, show yourself to the priest and offer the sacrifices that Moses commanded for your cleansing, as a testimony to them." (Mark 1:44)

Indeed, Paul further echoes the words of Jesus when he calls for us to make it our "ambition to lead a quiet life."

Make it your ambition to lead a quiet life, to mind your own business and to work with your hands, just as we told you. (1 Thessalonians 4:11)

Dreams and visions are just "straw" in the Lord compared to an obedient life. In fact, a crucified life is far more rare and important than all the miracles sweeping the world in the name of Jesus.

"Let the prophet who has a dream tell his dream, but let the one who has my word speak it faithfully. For what has straw to do with grain?" declares the Lord. (Jeremiah 23:28)

The Psalmists

Jesus reflected that we must first meditate on the Law and God's commands before getting excited about the wonders of God.

Let me understand the teaching of your precepts; then I will meditate on your wonders. (Psalms 119:27)

Pentecost was loud and came with fire, but ended in holy silence as each person thought about how to repent. It did not end in an emotional high or a manifestation of miracles, but everyone listening to a sermon. The sermon came as a result of God manifesting the miracle, not Peter preaching and calling for miracles.

Peter didn't advertise, "Come get your miracle," in order to fill the church.

> When the people heard this, they were cut to the heart and said to Peter and the other apostles, "Brothers, what shall we do?" (Acts 2:37)

Like Peter, we must preach a message of repentance, not miracles. If God chooses to work some miracles, great, but we must not preach miracles. To do so is a sign of a wicked and adulterous generation. If we walk away from a sermon about Jesus remembering the miracles, we missed everything. Many, like the nine lepers after having received their miracle, may not come back and surrender all to Jesus. Let it not be our fault because we preached miracles rather than the message of the cross.

Look to Jesus. He did a miracle then calmed the crowds down. The current crop of miracle workers do the complete opposite. They work the crowds up emotionally and leave them charged up. It is the same spirit one can find at a sporting event or a motivational meeting. Jesus always left the people sober minded and quiet in spirit, He never worked people up in order to perform a miracle. Such methods of performing miracles result in the short term influences of the mind over the body or demonic manifestations, not the power of God. The "horrible and shocking" part about this miracle madness is that not only are "lies" being preached but the church rules by its "own authority." Sure the church boasts of its authority in Christ, but it is really its own authority supported by Satan, just as the beast will support the dragon.

> Men worshiped the dragon because he had given authority to the beast, and they also worshiped the beast and asked, "Who is like the beast? Who can make war against him?" (Revelation 13:4)

Shocking Deception

Step back for a moment, isn't all this miracle madness "shocking."

134

A horrible and shocking thing has happened in the land: The
prophets prophesy lies, the priests rule by their own authority,
and my people love it this way. But what will you do in the end?
(Jeremiah 5:30–31)

What was "shocking" in the nation of Israel now happens on a
worldwide scale. It is "horrible" to behold the prophecies, dreams,
visions, and miracles invading the church which in reality are "lies."
Prideful preachers rule by their "own authority." Man-made love,
worship, and idolatry of miracles saturates multitudes of churches.
Miracles, however, without going to Jerusalem to die, leave men
open to false Christs and false prophets. They tell the people what
their flesh wants to hear and confirm the lie with "signs and
miracles."

Nothing is more sinister in its deception than a lie nearest the
truth. The most dangerous false Christ bears a remarkable resemblance to the true Christ. A false prophet who quotes Scripture word
for word without the cross, makes the perfect "Christian" liar. There
is nothing more deceptive to the church than a lying preacher who
can quote the Bible and confirm it with a miracle.

These preachers want a Jesus without a cross or the crucified
life. Just as in Jesus' day, people will not welcome a Savior who
preaches and lives the message of the cross. A Christianity where
Jesus "resolutely set out for Jerusalem" will not be welcomed by
the vast majority who have experienced His miracles. "Because
he was heading for Jerusalem" the people wanted nothing to do
with Jesus. A Jesus of the cross and with a cross simply is not
welcome in most churches and ministries today. It was this way
when Jesus walked the earth and truer today now that the tree is
dry.[2]

As the time approached for him to be taken up to heaven, Jesus
resolutely set out for Jerusalem. And he sent messengers on
ahead, who went into a Samaritan village to get things ready for
him; but the people there did not welcome him, because he was
heading for Jerusalem. (Luke 9:51–53)

A False Christ

So it will be in the last days, those who follow Jesus to the cross to die will not be welcomed in very many places. Surprisingly people rejected Jesus in places where He performed most of His miracles. God allows this false Jesus, this anti-Jesus who is like Jesus in every way, except for the cross, to confirm his teaching with miracles. Their ministry territory expands, miracles happen, and blessings abound, but God's judgment hides in it all.

> For false Christs and false prophets will appear and perform great signs and miracles to deceive even the elect—if that were possible. See, I have told you ahead of time. (Matthew 24:24–25)

A false Christ is at work when ministries focus on miracles to "win souls to Christ." A false prophet is at work when God's blessings motivate people to come to church rather than the offense of the cross; when waves of miracles are confused and equated with the Holy Spirit; when there's an implication that someone will be blessed if they come to God, and the blessings are worldly in nature; when those miracles are separate in nature and purpose from being crucified to self and hating one's life.

Get your blessing! Receive your anointing! Have your dreams come true! Come see God working in miracles! is the voice of sin calling in our churches today—insanity's seductive voice. The Powerful Delusion moves along with confirmation from miracles, signs, and wonders. We promote it on TV, radio, and in print. God did not permit Paul to tell of the miraculous heavenly visions he experienced. But today we shout such things from the rooftops with all the gusto self can muster.[3] We even make up miracles, dreams, and visions in our "Christian" novels and movies while Paul was given a "thorn in the flesh" to keep him from such pride.[4] Many a church could use a God-sent demon to "torment" them to deal with their pride.

The effects and influence of the Powerful Delusion leaves no one safe. It is easy to see God's wisdom in leaving many countries under authoritarian government controls. For those governments' attempts to keep out Christianity serve to protect those countries from the Powerful Delusion that seizes free Christian nations. However, even that barrier begins to fall as these governments don't mind letting in this false, crossless Christianity. Why do you think so many American ministries can expand their territory and influence? Obviously Satan has no reason to oppose them.

Increasing Miracles

Without the accompanying miracles, men would not so easily accept the false doctrines and twisting of God's Word. One can look back over time and see that as the church ignored and twisted Scriptures the miracles increased in our generation. As teachers reduce the message of the cross to a simple salvation call, the weirdness of miracles and pleasing the flesh grew in intensity. Now instead of just being slain in the Spirit, people experience "holy laughter," something unheard of years ago. A short time ago such behavior would have been equal with demon possession, yet today is considered a blessing from the Holy Ghost. The desire for greater and greater things that tantalize the flesh grows as men refuse the crucifying work of the cross. Instead of mourning in Jesus we now speak of "holy laughter."[5] One false doctrine and pleasing of self gives rise to another, just as in an insane asylum, where the madness of one inflames the madness in another.

The "false prophets" Jesus warned us about will perform "great signs and miracles." So great in power, intensity, and variety these miracles would deceive even the elect if it were not for the grace of God. As we approach the end days, the power of those signs and miracles will continue to grow and only those filled with the true grace of God will escape.

We live in a time when this Powerful Delusion sweeps the world and floods the church that lays claim to Jesus. Men embrace the delusions of mental illness and reject the truth of the gospel. This delusion comes with fire, zeal, joy, noise, and great excitement. It overwhelms individuals with miracles, signs, and wonders. It comes quoting Scripture, but in the spirit of Satan. It puffs up religious men and lifts ministries very high in the church. Just as some mental patients think themselves invincible, so too the false church speaks of overcoming Satan while he pulls the strings.

Presence of God or Satan?

They refuse to love the truth that calls for a man to lose and hate his life, wife, sons and daughters.[6] A cross is preached but the offense of the cross removed. Satan rejoices in a cross that does not offend the flesh of man unto death[7] and he gladly gives his support for messages that flatter religious self even as it points to Jesus.

As the false church prays for revival and the presence of God, a demon has met them. The demon speaks of Jesus and declares that their church proclaims the Truth, the way to be saved and they are flattered into apostasy. Remember, the beginning influence of the anti-Christ is found in flattery.

> With flattery he will corrupt those who have violated the covenant, but the people who know their God will firmly resist him. (Daniel 11:32)

Let's learn a lesson from the story in Acts about a demonic girl who met the disciples as they went to pray. Today's church would label the fortune-telling ability of this girl as prophecy. As these individuals foretell the future, or have insight about things happening in lives, they falsely think God works the good. After the Powerful Delusion has done its job what these individuals foretell will very often take place. Since this spirit feeds our spiritual flesh we think God blesses us when really demons deceive us.

Just as the girl in Acts earned a "great deal of money," so too the deluded church no longer knows how to hate and despise money. They have instead fallen in love with the bewitching spell that money casts. The way of the cross concerning money has been abandoned in order to fill the offering basket and their pockets. Satan all too happily attends such prayer meetings, for if the flattery works, though the message speaks of Jesus, it all comes back to Satan and self.

As you encounter this miracle of the slave girl, notice her truthful proclamation about Paul. "This girl followed Paul and the rest of us, shouting, 'These men are servants of the Most High God, who are telling you the way to be saved.'" That statement is the absolute truth, but from the wrong spirit. It does not have the spirit of the cross in it.

The girl flattered Paul and he knew it. Unfortunately, many in the church today cannot discern the flattery and would hold this girl up as someone spiritual. Right now someone in your church probably flatters others with the Truth and everyone views him or her as a spiritual person. This is the work of the Powerful Delusion.

> Once when we were going to the place of prayer, we were met by a slave girl who had a spirit by which she predicted the future. She earned a great deal of money for her owners by fortune-telling. This girl followed Paul and the rest of us, shouting, "These men are servants of the Most High God, who are telling you the way to be saved." (Acts 16:16–17)

Are not many miracle services filled with shouting and noise? Though this girl was "shouting" that Paul preached the truth and declared the way to be saved, it all pointed back to self. How easily we are taken in by demons that flatter us and our ministries. One can only wonder and shudder at the possibility of how many demon-inspired individuals stand in the church telling others how to be saved.[8] How deluded many remain as Satan sends demonic men and women to prayer meetings. The people in attendance really think that these individuals follow God. These ministries and churches remain happy to have someone building up their ministry and confirming it to others. The love of numbers and miracles that confirm us as spiritual, works its deluding influence. Since they preach themselves, they cannot see that the demonic girl was influenced by demons.

Misusing Scripture

Only those who know how to hate their lives by the power of the Holy Spirit will escape this very Powerful Delusion. For if there is one thing demons hate, it is the cross of Christ. Those performing miracles quote Scripture after Scripture about God's miraculous power. Indeed, Satan himself quotes Scripture, but removes the cross so that we will jump to our damnation. He uses Scripture in context to preach a lie. Satan will quote Scripture word for word if the power of the cross is not present. We have forgotten that ink on paper is not the Truth,[9] we must have the Holy Spirit to understand the Scriptures. And to have the Holy Spirit we must allow the Holy Spirit to crucify our flesh. Most are not willing to pay the price for such insight. This makes them easy pawns for Satan. For no matter how much Scripture Satan quotes, his spirit is always wrong which makes it all a lie. Remember, what Jesus said about the Truth?

> Yet a time is coming and has now come when the true worshipers will worship the Father in spirit and truth, for they are the kind of worshipers the Father seeks. God is spirit, and his worshipers must worship in spirit and in truth." (John 4:23–24)

In order to have the Truth, to honestly worship God, we must come to God in "spirit and truth." To put this in worldly terms, the spirit of the law must match the letter of the law. For example, the law states that we drive the speed limit and the police use their authority to ensure people obey the law. What if a policeman pulled someone over for speeding and insisted on giving him or her a ticket even though they were taking someone to the hospital having a heart attack? If the person died, we would blame the policeman because he misused the spirit, or intent of the law. The policeman misused the law to assert his authority for his own satisfaction of power.

Again, no matter how much Scripture Satan quotes, his spirit is always wrong. For this reason Paul rebuked the Corinthian church for putting up with a "different spirit." For the same reason

Jesus would not let demons tell who He was—they were of the wrong spirit even if they spoke the truth.

> For if someone comes to you and preaches a Jesus other than the Jesus we preached, or if you receive a different spirit from the one you received, or a different gospel from the one you accepted, you put up with it easily enough. (2 Corinthians 11:4)

Certainly the Scriptures teach that God moves powerfully and miraculously in our lives, but Truth is not found in how logically a man can apply ink on paper, or what we call the Bible. Because of our bad hearts, we do not concern ourselves with the spirit in our logic, rather we equate logic with truth. And because we are unwilling to pay the price to have a good heart to understand the truth, we become ripe for the Powerful Delusion. Christians have not died to self to allow the Holy Spirit to speak the Truth of God's miracles through the Bible. Without enlightenment from the Holy Spirit we cannot understand a single word in the Bible.[10] Without the cross, we use Scripture for our own selfish ends and become Satan's puppets as we go to our prayer meetings and miracle revivals. The false church fully embraces and loves the temptation of quoting Scripture apart from the cross. We fall for the temptation of being lifted up in the church just as the "devil" tried to tempt Jesus to perform a miracle apart from God.

> Then the devil took him to the holy city and had him stand on the highest point of the temple. "If you are the Son of God," he said, "throw yourself down. For it is written: "He will command his angels concerning you, and they will lift you up in their hands, so that you will not strike your foot against a stone." (Matthew 4:5–6)

Satan lifts up many churches and individuals in the "temple." Satan takes ministers and churches to the "highest point" of spiritual works, miracles, prophecies, religious feelings, and quotes Scripture. Note well that the Scripture is in context, but Satan quotes it. In the same way, many who sit in our pews quote the Bible out of pride and self.

The Scripture Satan quoted speaks of God's love, "He will command his angels concerning you," and protection, "so that you will not strike your foot against a stone." Satan whispers in our ears and shouts through false preachers that God will not punish us, nor send us to hell. The lie is being told over and over again and in the last days Satan will say "jump" and millions will obey.

Men love their opinions and insanity too much to die to self and be united in Christ. Many latch onto Scripture, laws, principles, miracles, and spiritual feelings thinking they can jump off the temple and be saved. Many will die and come to a surprise ending in hell, all because they refused to love the Spirit and Truth, the message of the cross that offends our flesh by the power of the Holy Spirit. God permits Satan to do this work because the church has rejected the narrow road gospel.

Letting Go of Self

Here's one small example. What started out as the false doctrine of being slain in the Spirit has permitted the rise of huge false ministries. After all, in Scripture the only people slain in the Spirit were those who came to oppose Jesus.

> So Judas came to the grove, guiding a detachment of soldiers and some officials from the chief priests and Pharisees. They were carrying torches, lanterns and weapons. Jesus, knowing all that was going to happen to him, went out and asked them, "Who is it you want?" "Jesus of Nazareth," they replied. "I am he," Jesus said. (And Judas the traitor was standing there with them.) When Jesus said, "I am he," they drew back and fell to the ground. (John 18:3–6)

Scripture speaks of others overcome by the Spirit, crucified more to self, and left devastated by the weakness and sinfulness of the flesh. But notice that no where in Scripture does a man ever cause another man to fall down. Men in the Bible fell only when God came to them and caught them by surprise. As we saw in the first chapter, Paul never used such gimmicks to draw people to his ministry. For he did not preach himself, but Jesus, therefore he had no need for the spectacular. When we preach ourselves, the need for more and more theatrics, miracles, and outward manifestations increases. For not only are we in competition with others, but we need new assurances repeatedly that we preach the truth.

> For we do not preach ourselves, but Jesus Christ as Lord, and ourselves as your servants for Jesus' sake. (2 Corinthians 4:5)

If we expect to stop idolizing miracles and falling prey to the Powerful Delusion then we must stop preaching and being concerned about ourselves.

Miracles Denounce Truth

Since the church has become very sensual, people use miracles to test whether something is of God or not. Feelings have replaced the cross. Those who carry their cross are discredited by false dreams and visions.

Twenty years ago, when I first started preaching the message of the cross, the hostility mainly came out in indifference. People felt self-satisfied and self-righteous in the their walk with God. They were so self-assured they reacted coldly to any question of the lie they lived. Their attitude was, "That is ok for you, but I am fine." They basically, with a little frustration, went their own way.

Not so today. The Powerful Delusion and insanity in the church has been so effective, the message of hating our lives meets only hostility. There has been a drastic, horrible change in the land and in the people claiming to know Jesus.

Now we meet people who have dreams and visions declaring the message of the cross to be wrong and a lie. Before we had met or they had much time to digest what we teach, great anger arises. False dreams and visions pour into the church. Since the cross that can test and reveal the truth about the dreams has been rejected, men are left to their own reasoning and feelings. And Satan all too happily declares in their ears that the dream is true.

Since men's feelings, beliefs, opinions, and experiences have become the proof of a truth or lie, Satan has free reign. The false church has fast become a church that receives truth by what it experiences, rather than receiving Truth by dying to the flesh on the cross. People now often talk about getting a bad "feeling," about a ministry as if those feelings were confirmation of truth. When reading my first book about the message of the cross, people almost universally say they get a bad feeling about it. Some persevere and find the freedom of the cross, while others reject the cross because they love themselves more than God.

Our flesh has been in charge for so long that any thought of crucifying the flesh makes us very nervous. In fact, the Garden of Eden had everything to do with feelings, how things looked and what was pleasing to the eye, so it is natural to look for churches that appeal to us. It comes natural to seek out a church that gives wisdom and makes the flesh feel comfortable. When the message of the cross is presented, the flesh feels threatened. Many do not get past this offense of the cross and allow the Truth to put them to death. At the same time, they don't want to go to hell, but rebel against the help that God offers. Times have changed so much that people have passed from just finding a church where they feel comfortable, to outright rage at the message of the cross because their flesh has experienced something—dream, miracle, feeling—confirming a lie.

The Oracle of the Lord

Man has been so lifted up and exalted in his opinions that everyone now feels something is of God just because they think it is so. And never has so much apostasy, twisting of Scripture, and using the Bible for selfish ends been so rampant. If anyone preaches by God's Spirit today, he will warn everyone to shut up and be extremely careful before saying, "Thus says the Lord."[11] For we live in desperate times when every man's opinion, commentary, and thoughts supposedly come from God. Liked-minded opinions form churches and since they all have the common element of self, soon these opinions come together as one opinion against the God who judges self. Jeremiah thoroughly rebuked this over-zealous love for prophecy and prophets, while in reality worshipping man's opinions.

> But you must not mention 'the oracle of the Lord' again, because every man's own word becomes his oracle and so you distort the words of the living God, the Lord Almighty, our God. This is what you keep saying to a prophet: 'What is the Lord's answer to you?' or 'What has the Lord spoken?' Although you claim, 'This is the oracle of the Lord,' this is what the Lord says: You used the words, 'This is the oracle of the Lord,' even though I told you that you must not claim, 'This is the oracle of the Lord.' (Jeremiah 23:36–38)

Two Choices

If you are part of the true church you can expect more and more individuals to experience dreams, visions, and miracles about your supposedly false Jesus. These experiences and confirmations will increase to the point that you must choose one of two camps. Either you will be in the camp where you honestly love God, or the camp that hates those who love God. Soon there will be no gray area, no middle ground. It will soon come down to two kinds of people. Those who hate their own lives and love Jesus, and those who hate those who hate their own lives for Jesus. You will either be hated by everyone or hate those who are true Christians. Either you will have overcome the Powerful Delusion, or you will have been overcome by it.

What a deadly, hellish combination this will be. The pride in man will become inflamed with unbridled lust for power to do miraculous things—that only Jesus himself can overcome when He returns. Truly "all" men will "hate" true Christians because of Jesus.

> All men will hate you because of me. (Luke 21:17)

Chapter 8

PLEASURE MADNESS

. . . lovers of pleasure rather than lovers of God— (2 Timothy 3:4)

- Come get your fun, food and salvation.
- Join our church for pack-the-pew day followed by an ice cream social.
- Attend our seminar, where we feature great speakers with recreational facilities and fine restaurants in the area.
- Come to a pig roast and baptism at the lake.
- Mothers' night out.
- Last days cruise in the Bahamas.
- Taco night, pizza night, movie night.
- Adventure Tuesday.
- Bowling, music, video games, and movies.
- Sports preview night.
- Men's prayer breakfast.
- Summer camp with us as we visit all the theme parks in the state.
- Big screen TV, swimming pool, a great time together.
- Church times will change to accommodate the Super Bowl.
- Two sanctuaries, one traditional the other with cappuccino and a big screen TV.

Look at any church bulletin and it is not hard to see how much the insanity of pleasure grips the church. The church is mad with the love of food and fun. Ads promote last days seminars that talk about the anti-Christ and the mark of the Beast while they brag about the eating, fun, and pleasurable things to do in the area. Everywhere you look the church is turning into one pleasure-mad social club, and with the stamp of approval called, "Fellowship."

No longer is the church a sanctuary from the pleasure and feasting of the world. Instead, Christians try to demonstrate that they can have fun too. The church stays too busy having fun to really do much of anything of value for Jesus. Certainly they perform token good deeds to feel spiritual, but never have a quiet, holy life separated from the world. Indeed, even if God were to speak in these busy, fun-filled churches, they could never hear Him—there is just too much noise.

One whitewash justification of such madness is to invite people to church by offering them fun and food so we can share Jesus with them. In reality, such offers entice and tempt people to come to church, something Jesus never did. Satan, on the other hand, did offer such pleasure in the garden of Eden.

Satan's Trap

Man fell over food. In order to cause sin, Satan tempted Adam and Eve to first look at the fruit in the garden. He enticed them to come to his church. Once they turned to go into Satan's church, they saw the "fruit" was "good for food and pleasing to the eye."

First, the church gets people's attention by saying the key words, "Fun and food." Once they get to church they discover it isn't so bad, in fact, the food is "good" and pleases "the eye." The false church is a "good" thing and fun to attend. It even gives a person "wisdom," as did the fruit at Satan's church. This "wisdom" looks and sounds godly, but only an outward form of being religious.

Satan works this appeal for pleasure with great speed in the last days. Notice the elements of Adam and Eve's first worldly church service:

- They "saw" they could obtain "wisdom" about life. They could see the power and authority to Satan's message. There was something different about this church.
- They saw that it was "good" food, making one healthy with a well-put-together life. It felt personally "good" for them to go to church, and enriched their spiritual life.
- It was "pleasing" to attend, it was fun and felt good. Eve had a good feeling about what she did. It didn't look like a cult or some weird group. It made one feel spiritual and comfortable.
- It was "desirable" and they wanted to attend church. They couldn't wait to get to this church service.
- It even focused on evangelism with Eve giving "some to her husband." At this church everyone reached out to the needs and wants of others.
- It was contemporary, meeting the needs of the moment.
- And of course a woman did the preaching. She now fulfilled her calling, using her new found wisdom to influence Adam into following in her footsteps.

When the woman saw that the fruit of the tree was good for food and pleasing to the eye, and also desirable for gaining wisdom, she took some and ate it. She also gave some to her husband, who was with her, and he ate it. (Genesis 3:6)

Terrible Times

Of all the things Paul warned Timothy about the last days, nowhere did he mention earthquakes, wars, famines, or some bad political group. The "terrible times" we must "mark" or take note of, is a "form of" Christianity that claims to be godly but really loves pleasure. "Mark" well the things we have touched on in this book listed out in the next Scripture.

But mark this: There will be terrible times in the last days. People will be lovers of themselves, lovers of money, boastful, proud, abusive, disobedient to their parents, ungrateful, unholy, without love, unforgiving, slanderous, without self-control, brutal, not lovers of the good, treacherous, rash, conceited, lovers of pleasure rather than lovers of God—having a form of godliness but denying its power. Have nothing to do with them. (2 Timothy 3:1–5)

This Scripture says that the only safeguard from such churches, ministries, and works in the name of Jesus is to have "nothing to do with them." Let me repeat that, we, those who live the message of the cross, must have "nothing" to do with them. We need to do as Paul says and "mark this" or be prepared to take the mark of the Beast.

A Hungry Crowd

We must understand that Jesus did not promote His teachings, or a relationship with God, by saying "Come get your free food." In fact, the people did not even know Jesus planned to feed them. As we shall see they had followed Jesus all that distance, listened to his teachings about denying self and the love of God; they had gotten themselves so far out with Jesus that they would have "collapsed" on the journey home. This "large crowd" had listened to Jesus for "three days" with "nothing to eat." At this point, after days without food, Jesus told the disciples to give them something to eat. Jesus had not gotten the crowd out to Him by promising a fun filled, action packed, belly satisfying miracle revival time.

> During those days another large crowd gathered. Since they had nothing to eat, Jesus called his disciples to him and said, "I have compassion for these people; they have already been with me three days and have nothing to eat. If I send them home hungry, they will collapse on the way, because some of them have come a long distance." (Mark 8:1–3)

Until Jesus had them "sit down"[1] the crowd did not know what they would eat, and fun was the last thing on their minds. They were so busy feeding on what Jesus had to say, seeing how to hate their lives, that having fun never occurred to them. I remember when I first started the church in Washington state, most members had come out of a Powerful Delusion church, and pleasure and feeding the flesh came naturally. Everyone came to our first church services with coffee cups in their hands, passing out mints, and talking about food. I never rebuked them for this, but just preached the message of the cross as Jesus worked it. Naturally these activities and seeking to have pleasure all the time began to die away. I didn't lay down rules but just preached the gospel of loving God wholeheartedly and slowly the Holy Spirit began to do the work. Now we serve much simpler meals during our fellowship time and we talk less about feeding the belly and our plans for fun. Our Body has found their pleasure and food in doing the will of God—food most know "nothing about."[2]

Simple Meal

We should also take note that Jesus fed the people a simple meal of fish and bread. As all the people sat down on the plain "green grass,"[3] Jesus fed them a simple meal. The green grass was not used for golfing, sun bathing, or tables with cakes and fine foods, instead for contemplation and serious thought. Jesus did not promise the crowd a fun time or tell them that all their needs would be met. Indeed, the miracle happened so quietly that, most probably didn't know a miracle took place. Jesus simply said a very short prayer[4] to bless the food and thousands were fed. Contrast this with what happens today. We invite thousands to a miracle feeding time. Sitting down in "green grass" is not enough, we promise fun and food for all—a pot blessing. We bring out the insane clowns so the children do not get bored. We offer up long-winded prayers for God to work a miracle on the food. Lots of fun, music, and shouting keeps everyone hyped up. Certainly our church meals do not consist of simple fish and bread, but BBQ beef, ice cream topped with whip cream—all you can eat. In short, everyone has a really good time of "fellowship." How the church today defiles itself by eating the rich food of kings. Better to have a knife applied to the throat than to sin in the manner which takes place in most churches today. Let everyone "note well" what is put "before" them and if it be the rich food of a "ruler" and you are "given to gluttony," put the knife to your throat, not the food.

> When you sit to dine with a ruler, note well what is before you, and put a knife to your throat if you are given to gluttony. (Proverbs 23:1–2)

Lift Up Jesus

The vast crowd that claims to know Jesus seems willing to do about anything to get people into church. They constantly advertise in small and great styles that they provide fun, food, recreation, child-care, and a rich spiritual time for all—for a nominal fee of course, discounts for those who register early.

Again, the love of numbers and money motivates this corruption of fun and food. In fact, the reader might ask, "Well, then how can we get people to church? How can we win souls?" By now you know the answer—by the work of the cross. Preach the gospel, as the Holy Spirit instructs, and leave the drawing of men to God. We have used the worldly enticements and advertisements for so long that we have forgotten that the weakness of man allows the cross to do its work in the heart of man. Notice that Jesus said when we have "lifted him" up on the cross, He, not us, will "draw all men" to Himself.

> But I, when I am lifted up from the earth, will draw all men to myself. (John 12:32)

When we preach ourselves, we use worldly means to attract. When we rely fully on the Holy Spirit we know that only God can draw the heart, and all we can do is "water" or "plant." In short, all we can do in our human effort is appeal to an individual's flesh. Therefore we must die to that flesh and rely on God to do the work. For this reason, Scripture draws a distinction between those who believe in Jesus by the effort of man and those who believe by "grace."[5] It is God's work to "open" the "hearts" of people to His gospel, not man's responsibility.[6]

True Altar Calls

Plus, think about it. Does it really make sense to entice people to come to the Lord using entertainment and food, and then tell them they must "hate their own life," "deny self," and pick up a cross? After all, how can a man count the cost when the church that represents Jesus requires so little and when the cleaning up of one's life includes no more than what the world expects or demands. We very seldom present Jesus' true altar call. We motivate people in the power of the flesh by singing "Just As I am" over and over until we get the desired response. Our flesh loves bringing people to God through the "Romans Road," ask-Jesus-in-your-heart, sign the back of the book, raise your hand, speak in tongues, or attend discipleship class methods. We write off Luke 14 as if it means "love less," and think that if we love other things less than God, then it is okay to have other loves.

So many millions become Christians while having many loves (idols), in their lives. The end-time church has lost most of its "saltiness" and will soon be "thrown out" into darkness. All gospel calls that do not reflect the Scripture below will be thrown out. For a detailed look at Luke 14:26, read my book *The Essential Piece*. For now, let us underscore that when Jesus confronts us it causes all to "sit down" and do some very serious contemplation. Jesus turns to the "large crowds" in churches and declares the following:

> Large crowds were traveling with Jesus, and turning to them he said: "If anyone comes to me and does not hate his father and mother, his wife and children, his brothers and sisters—yes, even his own life—he cannot be my disciple. And anyone who does not carry his cross and follow me cannot be my disciple. "Suppose one of you wants to build a tower. Will he not first sit down and estimate the cost to see if he has enough money to complete it? For if he lays the foundation and is not able to finish it, everyone who sees it will ridicule him, saying, 'This

fellow began to build and was not able to finish.' "Or suppose a king is about to go to war against another king. Will he not first sit down and consider whether he is able with ten thousand men to oppose the one coming against him with twenty thousand? If he is not able, he will send a delegation while the other is still a long way off and will ask for terms of peace. In the same way, any of you who does not give up everything he has cannot be my disciple. "Salt is good, but if it loses its saltiness, how can it be made salty again? It is fit neither for the soil nor for the manure pile; it is thrown out. "He who has ears to hear, let him hear." (Luke 14:25–35)

Belly Belief

Jesus wants all of self crucified, not just some aspects of self cleaned up.[7] See the absurdity? The Powerful Delusion succeeds in making it seem holy to entice people with fun, entertainment, and food. Churches even make spiritual gifts appear fun in order to attract new members. The church must come to realize that they do not save souls, but prepare a people for God to judge and send to hell. A people, as Jesus said, "twice as much a son of hell as themselves."[8]

When push comes to shove those who embrace the Powerful Delusion do so because they use Jesus to puff up their ministry and to satisfy their flesh in many ways. They want God on their side in case something goes wrong; they do not want to go hungry or unsatisfied in this world. Jesus tells them in no uncertain terms that they look for Him, not really because of the "miraculous signs but because" they "ate the loves and had" their "fill." They follow Jesus for the free food and fun. Jesus added a little more excitement to their life and their flesh liked it.

Many go on short missionary trips just for this reason. It makes them feel spiritual and adds a little more spice to their lives. But they do not follow Him in order to be fit for the kingdom of heaven. They are belly believers who follow Jesus because their faith is for their stomachs. Indeed, such believers call others brothers, but they are really just belly brothers in the name of Jesus. They have a belly belief as described in the book of Philippians.

> Join with others in following my example, brothers, and take note of those who live according to the pattern we gave you. For, as I have often told you before and now say again even with tears, many live as enemies of the cross of Christ. Their destiny is destruction, their god is their stomach, and their glory is in their shame. Their mind is on earthly things. (Philippians 3:17–19)

Paul gave them a pattern of denying self, being crucified to self, and suffering on the cross to be dead to sin. He taught how to be dead to the world and know that food was for the "stomach and the stomach for food."[9] Paul spoke of a cross that separated us from the pleasures and fun in the world so that we might enjoy life with Christ for eternity.[10] Paul considered the cross such a treasure that he wrote these words with "tears" and pleaded with us to "take note" of those living the crucified life. How many churches are "enemies of the cross of Christ" as evidenced by how they misuse food and fun. Their lives declare what they really worship even though they mock the words of the cross.

Look again at the crowd following Jesus. They were eager to find Jesus and put forth great effort searching for Him. They felt excited to find Jesus and asked, "Rabbi, when did you get here?" They come calling Him "Rabbi" or Teacher. They come with false respect and false sincerity undetectable to even themselves. Just like millions in the church today, they pack the pews and call Jesus "Lord," but all with wrong motives and desires.

> Once the crowd realized that neither Jesus nor his disciples were there, they got into the boats and went to Capernaum in search of Jesus. When they found him on the other side of the lake, they asked him, "Rabbi, when did you get here?" Jesus answered, "I tell you the truth, you are looking for me, not because you saw miraculous signs but because you ate the loaves and had your fill. Do not work for food that spoils, but for food that endures to

eternal life, which the Son of Man will give you. On him God the Father has placed his seal of approval." (John 6:24–27)

Jesus told them they only looked for Him so they could get something from Him. The "miraculous signs" attracted the crowd as they hoped to get something for themselves and claim a miracle for their life. Jesus fed their bellies and made their lives easier, therefore they looked for Him. For the same reason we see mega-churches today and flourishing ministries—they feed the bellies of men and women. Many signs, wonders, feelings, and a sense of spirituality confirms this belly belief. The Powerful Delusion happens before our eyes as we promise people great things in the name of Jesus.

Share in His Suffering

No greater question can a man ask himself in our time period than this: Why do I follow Jesus? Do I follow in spite of the sufferings of the cross, or do I follow to try and get away from the sufferings of the world?

We are discussing a true cross that takes all of a man's life, not a cross that delivers a person from the sufferings of Christ. For only those who suffer with Christ are children of God. Only those who suffer with sin and overcome will live with Jesus in heaven.[11] Everyone else lives a delusion and the Powerful Delusion seeds live in their hearts.

> Now if we are children, then we are heirs—heirs of God and co-heirs with Christ, if indeed we share in his sufferings in order that we may also share in his glory. (Romans 8:17)

Festival to the Lord?

If a man can discern the golden-calf worship happening on a large scale, there is hope he might pick up a cross unto salvation. As Moses came down off the mountain with the wonderful Law of God in his hands, he found sin in the camp. Let us remember what the Israelites experienced. They were a people delivered, separated, and soon to become priests. They experienced miracles and divine revelation and were declared a special people. However God was not pleased with them,[12] and they perished just outside the promised land. Let us jump in and view this revealing moment.

As Moses descended the sound of the camp filled his ears, and he heard the sound of great "fellowship." The people had become restless and bored and went off in search of a power-packed worship time. Indeed, many today feel bored with traditional church services, which is a direct sign of golden calf worship.

> The tablets were the work of God; the writing was the writing of God, engraved on the tablets. When Joshua heard the noise of the people shouting, he said to Moses, "There is the sound of war in the camp." Moses replied: "It is not the sound of victory, it is not the sound of defeat; it is the sound of singing that I hear." (Exodus 32:16–18)

Moses descends the mountain with Joshua carrying the "work of God" in his hands, but the people became too bored to wait. Joshua heard the sound of war and Moses declared it was "singing." Both were correct, a spiritual battle was taking place and one group chose to have a little fun. Like in Moses' day, today's spiritual battle comes with singing and shouting all in the name of the Lord. Its musicians look, speak, and act like the world, and boast of trying to crossover to the secular market, thus making themselves enemies of God.[13] Today golden calf worship music comes shrink wrapped in the name of revival music. Church services in reality are just stage productions rather than true worship. All of this insanity in the church comes in the name of the Lord but comes from the pit of hell. Like Aaron, rather than calling people to repentance, we whitewash their sin and call it a "festival to the Lord."

> When Aaron saw this, he built an altar in front of the calf and announced, "Tomorrow there will be a festival to the Lord." (Exodus 32:5)

It was a "festival to the Lord" in name only. The real motivation, the real god, what they really worshiped was their stomachs. Their whole goal was to sit down and eat, then get up and play. They "indulge[d] in revelry" after they sang songs and praised God.

> Afterward they sat down to eat and drink and got up to indulge in revelry. (Exodus 32:6)

First, they got "church" out of the way. They sacrificed "burnt offerings" and presented "fellowship offerings." Their offerings came with fire and sacrifice, looking so holy as they raised arms to God. I'm sure they talked about where they planned to eat after the sermon. If possible, they would have had a coffee shop in the lobby and their church calendar would have been dated with one fun event after another. People lined up "early" to get a good seat at this church for golden calf worship, which is called a revival service today.

> So the next day the people rose early and sacrificed burnt offerings and presented fellowship offerings. Afterward they sat down to eat and drink and got up to indulge in revelry. (Exodus 32:6)

The people "rose early," did the church thing, sat down to eat, and then got up to play, all in the name of the Lord. It was a corruption of God's ways, with elements of Truth and worship, and we see it in abundance today as the Powerful Delusion does its deadly work.

> Then the Lord said to Moses, "Go down, because your people, whom you brought up out of Egypt, have become corrupt. They have been quick to turn away from what I commanded them and have made themselves an idol cast in the shape of a calf. They have bowed down to it and sacrificed to it and have said, 'These are your gods, O Israel, who brought you up out of Egypt.' "I have seen these people," the Lord said to Moses, "and they are a stiff-necked people. (Exodus 32:7–9)

Promoting the Lie

As the Powerful Delusion settles more and more on the church today, the number of "stiff-necked people" increases. People become increasingly hardened to the Truth and in the end persecute those who know the way of the cross. Indeed, my first book about the message of the cross was thoroughly slandered by a group that shows others the way to believe the Lie. They stand at the forefront of the Powerful Delusion and it is natural they would fight against the message of the cross. Indeed, God works in their lives and allows Satan to confirm the Powerful Delusion. They have the numbers and the money to promote the Lie in ways unheard of before our time. After all it is easy to get people to sacrifice and give when the golden calf of self is fed.

> When the people saw that Moses was so long in coming down from the mountain, they gathered around Aaron and said, "Come, make us gods who will go before us. As for this fellow Moses who brought us up out of Egypt, we don't know what has happened to him." Aaron answered them, "Take off the gold earrings that your wives, your sons and your daughters are wearing, and bring them to me." (Exodus 32:1-2)

Feed the people's flesh and they will "take off the gold earrings" that their "wives," "sons" and "daughters" wear. After all, who doesn't want to give to a good cause that feeds your flesh. What men will not sacrifice for Jesus by way of the cross, they will sacrifice for self in the name of Jesus. When fun and food are a goal men will sacrifice much. With great care these preachers and leaders will fashion something that will please the eye of man, look spiritual, and have a lot of fun to it.

In our time, tongues, healings, being slain in the Spirit, miracles, signs, wonders, dreams, and visions have become our golden calves. They give new pleasures to eating and drinking and having fun because the cross is absent. Even those who did not go for the outlandish things still like the food and spicy worship. Moderate sinners in the church have a false sense of security because they are not like the wild bunch.

For example, tongues, while a genuine gift for today, has become an idol. So much so that you cannot preach in a certain denomination if you don't speak in tongues. Even the youngest children are told to practice speaking in tongues. This denomination believes the sign of being filled with the Holy Spirit manifests by speaking in tongues. This idolatry, which started out small, ushered into the church such things as barking in the Spirit, holy laughter, and other nonsense. Combine this with fun and food and it becomes a very deadly mix of worldliness. There is nothing worse than a man puffed up in self-righteous zeal confirmed by outward manifestations that confirm his lies and delusions.

Sexual Immorality

These false manifestations are "fashioned" with great excitement, promotion, and zeal. We call it a revival meeting but God still sees it as golden calf worship. Deep inside many preachers of today know all these styles of worship are false and ungodly. Many preachers declare this hype false, but if they do not allow it they will lose members, popularity, money, and their reputation. All of this love for fun and food has led to unprecedented sexual immorality and godlessness.

If we had the eyes of Jesus we would see millions sell their birthright in Jesus for a "single meal." You don't have to be a dancing golden calf worshipper to have sold your heritage in the Lord. Many times it all comes down to a single, simple meal. Just as it did for Esau.

> See that no one is sexually immoral, or is godless like Esau, who for a single meal sold his inheritance rights as the oldest son. (Hebrews 12:16)

Few people today "see that no one" falls into this sin in the church. People are told over and over not to judge and to be more loving, so no one is permitted to "See that no one is . . ." We don't have time to examine how eating and drinking link with sexual immorality, but the church gives the perfect example. As the eating, drinking, and fun increase, so does sexual immorality. Indeed, if we had eyes that could see behind the scenes, we would be appalled at the sexual immorality taking place. If what we can see is this bad, one can only shudder at what God will do when He exposes the hidden behavior. For now just look at the dress, conduct, eating, and drinking that goes on in the church—it is appalling how far the church has fallen.

King's Kids

If you do not think this is true, just look at the church bulletins or read ads placed in magazines that advertise revival and seminars. Take a day and just listen to what others talk about in church. See how much conversation has to do with fun and food. The usual questions of the day at church services is, "Where are you going to go eat?" or "What do are you going to do today?"

The church has grown arrogant and prideful, boasting repeatedly that its members are kids of the King. How little the church knows today that Satan tempts it, so dull are the souls of men in the church. As Satan came to Jesus saying, "If you are the Son of God" eat. So too Satan comes to the church saying, "If you are a child of the King, then it is your right to eat, drink and be free in Jesus." We, however, eat when Jesus did not.

> The tempter came to him and said, "If you are the Son of God, tell these stones to become bread." Jesus answered, "It is written: 'Man does not live on bread alone, but on every word that comes from the mouth of God.'" (Matthew 4:3–4)

Cleansing Drink

To escape this insanity, one must begin to swing the sword of the Lord. Not a physical sword, but the sword of the living Word of God that reveals such false worship and motives as sin. Just like in Moses' day, you must decide, is this cross stuff correct or not?

Which side will you go with, for there is no middle ground on this issue? We must do what Moses did to purify the church.

Let every preacher everywhere stop the dancing and show the people how they have broken the work of God into "pieces." Let the sin be looked at clearly and focused on until it is but a "powder." Then let us put this sin in cleansing "water" and make the people "drink" it until they understand. Grind the gold, shiny, attractive sin so fine until the blood of Jesus purifies it. For this is exactly what Moses did.

If you grind gold into a very fine powder it will turn water blood red when mixed together. Indeed, even doctors use finely ground gold for healing purposes. The blood of Jesus is more precious than gold and when God strikes at our sin, no matter how shiny that sin, if we apply the blood of Jesus it heals.

> When Moses approached the camp and saw the calf and the dancing, his anger burned and he threw the tablets out of his hands, breaking them to pieces at the foot of the mountain. And he took the calf they had made and burned it in the fire; then he ground it to powder, scattered it on the water and made the Israelites drink it. (Exodus 32:19–20)

To escape this delusion one must drink deeply of confession for this sin. We must "drink it" before the Lord if we hope to be cleansed and forgiven of our love of pleasure. No casual repentance will cure the church of this sin. Every excuse must be dealt with that causes the corruption to get out of hand. We must expose and rebuke the Aarons in the church today. Church leaders must demolish every pretension and argument used to justify sin and grind them to a fine powder. The argument of justification must be stripped of its power, as the gold was stripped off the calf.

> He said to Aaron, "What did these people do to you, that you led them into such great sin?" "Do not be angry, my lord," Aaron answered. "You know how prone these people are to evil. They said to me, 'Make us gods who will go before us. As for this fellow Moses who brought us up out of Egypt, we don't know

what has happened to him.' So I told them, 'Whoever has any gold jewelry, take it off.' Then they gave me the gold, and I threw it into the fire, and out came this calf!" (Exodus 32:21–24)

Nothing "Just Happens"

The love of pleasure must be exposed and rebuked. Look at how Aaron minimized this sin just as the church does today. He made it sound like this thing just happened and was a "God thing." He declared, "I threw it into the fire, and out came this calf!" Aaron never admitted to planning, building, or fashioning to prepare the food and the idol. How the church likes to make such foolishness sound like it just happens, but in reality carefully plans such events.

The sin of pleasure in the church doesn't just happen, people plan it. In fact, people love to plan a golden calf church service full of fun. There is nothing more fun than being on a golden calf committee. Who doesn't want to plan how to have fun in the name of the Lord? Golden calf worship produces quick, easy unity, but unity by the cross is slow, hard, and laborious. Men don't want to pay the price for holiness. Let those willing to stand at the door of the church say with Moses, "Whoever is for the Lord, come to me," and then set out to destroy the golden calves.

As you read the passage below notice how Moses was also concerned because Aaron let the church become a group of fools, a "laughingstock to their enemies." When people look at the church today their reaction is laughter, and rightly so. Too many insane men preach from the pulpits. Too many people dance around a golden calf for the world to take a few true Christians seriously.

> Moses saw that the people were running wild and that Aaron had let them get out of control and so become a laughingstock to their enemies. So he stood at the entrance to the camp and said, "Whoever is for the Lord, come to me." And all the Levites rallied to him. (Exodus 32:25–26)

Let those who rally to the cross go throughout the camp looking for things that cause this sin. Let the righteous strike at the self

in the congregation and if their brother, friend, or neighbor refuses to repent, have nothing to do with them.

> Then he said to them, "This is what the Lord, the God of Israel,
> says: 'Each man strap a sword to his side. Go back and forth
> through the camp from one end to the other, each killing his
> brother and friend and neighbor.'" (Exodus 32:27)

God will call you "blessed" because you love the Lord more
than approval of men. By the way, the Levites became priests of
God because they stood against their brothers and sisters.

> The Levites did as Moses commanded, and that day about three
> thousand of the people died. Then Moses said, "You have been set
> apart to the Lord today, for you were against your own sons and
> brothers, and he has blessed you this day." (Exodus 32:28–29)

For all the boasting and bragging in churches about being priests
of God, people certainly do not stand against their "sons and brothers." After all, who wants to do this when you feel so blessed and
are having so much fun. Indeed, it is hard to fight a battle with
bellies so bloated and overfed. It is difficult indeed to have our
minds on things above when entertainment fills our thoughts. Just
as Moses found the people "running wild and out of control," we
too must put a stop to this insanity.

Chapter 9

ALTAR CALL MADNESS

. . . sit down and estimate the cost (Luke 14:28)

. . . sit down and consider (Luke 14:31)

- Jesus said "sit down," not dance around.
- Jesus said, "sit down," not take a count.
- Jesus said, "sit down," not get emotionally charged up.
- Jesus said "sit down," not "come on down."
- Jesus said, "sit down," not "write it down."

Altar call madness has replaced the gospel call of Christ. Jesus declared that we must "count the cost" and "estimate" what it means to become a "disciple." Indeed, Jesus didn't make Christians, He made disciples. But even the word disciple has taken on a new meaning since the invention of the modern day altar call. Because of altar call madness, the word disciple is used to sell study guides void of the offense of the cross.

Jesus did not tell people to just ask God into their heart, come on down, and get counted. He told the people to *count* the cost, not *be* counted. The modern altar call mixes all the elements of insanity. It provides a quick number count, contains emotionalism, and makes the gospel call easy, cheap, and showy. The musicians keep playing the songs over and over again until they obtain the desired result. Scripture does not contain a single reference to someone just "asking Jesus into their hearts." Instead something much more serious, narrow, and life changing happens.

Very little teaching left in the church causes anyone to "sit down" and think about what it means to be a Christian. Very few sermons leave individuals stunned at what it means to call oneself a Christian. Instead of sitting down in deep thought and contemplation, sermons motivate audiences to come to Christ by stirring up their emotions. The best way to illustrate the insanity of altar call madness is to describe how people became Christians in the days of Jesus, which I will do in the following composite. For a deeper discussion you may wish to obtain a copy of the book, *Even The Demons Believe.*[1]

A Composite of Salvation

Composites of Scripture can be a very dangerous thing, since they often remove the liberty of the Holy Spirit. Composites always fall short and cannot possibly convey the mind of God. Certainly I do not want to reduce this teaching down to steps, but for the sake of demonstrating this point, I will do so. With this caution in mind, this composite describes the event for an average person (if there is such a thing as an average person) to come to the Lord. Every scripture will be taken into consideration, though you, no doubt, will be able to add more of your own.

We will call the main character of our composite Joe Sinner. We prayed a long time for Joe Sinner to come to the Lord. Long before we came on the scene God used others to prepare his heart. Now at the crucial moment, someone comes along in the spirit of John the Baptist. If Joe Sinner will not accept this baptism of repentance, he will not accept the baptism of Jesus, which comes with fire later. You see, some folks, especially the religious ones, do not like the manner in which Jesus comes to them or the way in which He says certain things. Since they want their dignity and religiosity protected, they will not respond to the sternness of John.

Therefore those who will not respond to John will never accept Jesus. This explains why the Pharisees could not accept Jesus,

> But the Pharisees and experts in the law rejected God's purpose for themselves, because they had not been baptized by John. (Luke 7:30)

Because of John the Baptist, Joe Sinner begins to see many things he must stop doing in order for Jesus to get to Him. The valleys must be filled in, the mountains leveled, and the crooked roads in his life straightened out. In other words, he must begin to reject some things that get in the way of God reaching him. For example, he might choose to go to church on Wednesday night instead of working late at the office. Joe will rearrange his life so that Jesus can get to him. He might even climb a tree like Zacchaeus to see Jesus coming by.[2] Certainly, even this repentance comes from God, but let each man respond fully to the first weak impulses of the call of God in his life.[3]

We must stop what we are doing, go out to a John the Baptist who calls in the desert, and contemplate life. We need to see the meaninglessness of life and how quickly we must change. True salvation requires taking time for God and examining our lives. Joe Sinner must ask himself, "What can I do to respond to God?" This is no simple thing. It is a baptism or immersion in the things of God. This call brings a baptism of repentance and not a casual examination of religion or a study on the character of God. This repentance looks at the specific faults in a man's life. This will be Joe Sinner's first acknowledgment that he needs help. Although he does not realize just how much help he needs, it is nevertheless the starting place.

Repentance Call

Joe Sinner goes out to hear a preacher, and look at what greets him. He doesn't receive a nice warm "hello" and handshake from John and his congregation. He isn't given a nice visitor tag and made to feel welcome. No, John calls Joe, who already feels his need for God (otherwise he would not be in the desert) some kind of snake, a poisonous viper!

> John said to the crowds coming out to be baptized by him, "You brood of vipers! Who warned you to flee from the coming wrath? Produce fruit in keeping with repentance. And do not begin to say to yourselves, 'We have Abraham as our father.' For I tell you that out of these stones God can raise up children for Abraham. The ax is already at the root of the trees, and every tree that does not produce good fruit will be cut down and thrown into the fire." "What should we do then?" the crowd asked. John answered, "The man with two tunics should share with him who has none, and the one who has food should do the same." Tax collectors also came to be baptized. "Teacher," they asked, "what should we do?" (Luke 3:7–12)

Again notice how John acts. He calls the church visitors "vipers" and has one message that he repeats over and over again: "fruit." In fact, as Joe Sinner comes walking down the aisle to receive salvation, John stops him dead in his tracts and asks him, "Who warned you?" In other words, John says, "What makes you think you are ready for God's mercy?" Such a reaction to sinners coming forward is totally unheard of today, yet considered normal in the days of Jesus and John the Baptist.

Joe might at first think this sounds awfully legalistic and harsh. In fact he wonders why John never mentions love and mercy. He probably thinks this Baptist fellow goes a bit overboard with all that preaching on obedience and everything. Indeed John seems to put off, by being rude, the people wanting to come forward. John also seeks to destroy every religious pretense they have by saying, "Do not begin to say to yourself, 'We have Abraham.'"

Joe cannot figure out why John treats everyone so hard. He no doubt mumbles to himself that these people at least try to do the best they can. They support John's ministry and Joe can't figure out why the Baptist treats them so badly. He may even question if John understands the grace and mercy of God. I know from experience that if you don't kiss the babies and bend over backward thanking folks for coming to church, they become offended. Of course that does not bother me. For if they cannot stand not to have a little bit of attention paid to them, then what will they do when God comes to crucify them?

God uses servants of God to point out every failure and excuse a person has for not getting ready for Jesus. How many in the Church today stop the Spirit of God right at this point? Yet Jesus did this gently with the woman at the well when He pointed out all her sins,[4] and John, in God's way, did the same thing.

Get Ready for Jesus

This is just the beginning stage for a person to consider the meaning of Salvation so they can allow Jesus to purify him or her later. At times Jesus sends us out to get things ready for Him, but the message always calls for repentance and bearing fruit. It is always, "Get ready and make some changes now because Jesus is coming by."

> After this the Lord appointed seventy–two others and sent them two by two ahead of him to every town and place where he was about to go. (Luke 10:1)

> They went out and preached that people should repent. (Mark 6:12)

Notice, that the crowd ask John the same question that the crowd asked Peter on the day of Pentecost: "What should we do then?" It is the starting question God poses through John the Baptist and the finishing question just before salvation at Pentecost. The Powerful Delusion never drives a person to cry "What must I do?"

At This Point

God only gives the Holy Spirit to those who obey Him. Little wonder that God uses the John the Baptists of this world to get men ready for the baptism of fire that comes through Jesus.[5] For if they cannot handle John's easy preaching, they will never accept the purification that comes with the Holy Spirit.

At this point Joe Sinner begins to take steps to order his life; he constantly thinks of ways to prepare himself for Jesus. He even deals with the first mountain peaks of pride and the valleys of self-pity in his life. He looks for ways to straighten out the crooked roads in his life. As he acts upon these things, though weak as they might be, Jesus jumps in on the scene. While we usually have people accept the Lord as Savior right then and there, Jesus first has them walk with Him.

Although humbled at first, Joe Sinner, like the disciples, begins to walk with Jesus toward the cross. As he travels with Jesus, the discussions get deeper and the conviction becomes greater. The realization of Jesus becomes clearer because he learns about the character of Jesus. If Joe Sinner is a pagan, he is taught the basics of Christianity. If he had been a religious person, his beliefs are shattered. He studies and listens to sermons a lot at this stage. Joe might even see a miracle or two and experiences God working in his life to bless him. He may experience answered prayer for the first time.

Our Joe, however, has not yet arrived at a salvation point. With some people it may take a year or so to fully receive Christ. With others, like the thief on the cross, salvation comes only in a matter of hours. God knows the heart and you must listen to Him to know what to do with each person. Usually at this point "many" things must be taught and great amounts of "compassion" shown to Joe Sinner, all through the direction of the Holy Spirit.

> When Jesus landed and saw a large crowd, he had compassion on them, because they were like sheep without a shepherd. So he began teaching them many things. (Mark 6:34)

Elementary Teachings

Don't be surprised at all if many individuals agree with and like what they hear. At this point many join the Church and membership swells. Thus the "large crowd" comes into play and many become interested in the grace, power, and mercy of God. Multitudes of preachers like to keep their congregations (and their numbers and livelihood) at this stage.[6] Such men always preach the same basic elementary things over and over. Many times you can recognize such preachers by the fact that they always preach a salvation message. Such churches practice altar call madness and allow people to come forward time and time again.

Of course it isn't only the preachers' fault; the people also love it that way. They can hear a tough sermon about righteousness without really being crucified. They can appear white and clean while still not hating their own lives. The people and the preachers both love this whitewash. After all, whitewash is cheap, easy to apply, and gives a quick appearance of holiness. Unfortunately, it will not stand the test of God and in the end the people will complain in vain against such preachers.

> Because they lead my people astray, saying, "Peace," when there is no peace, and because, when a flimsy wall is built, they cover it with whitewash, therefore tell those who cover it with whitewash that it is going to fall. Rain will come in torrents, and I will send hailstones hurtling down, and violent winds will burst forth. When the wall collapses, will people not ask you, "Where is the whitewash you covered it with?" Therefore this is what the Sovereign Lord says: "In my wrath I will unleash a violent wind, and in my anger hailstones and torrents of rain will fall with destructive fury. I will tear down the wall you have covered with whitewash and will level it to the ground so that its foundation will be laid bare. When it falls, you will be destroyed in it; and you will know that I am the Lord. So I will spend my wrath against the wall and against those who covered it with whitewash. I will say to you, 'The wall is gone and so are those who whitewashed it, those prophets of Israel who prophesied to Jerusalem and saw visions of peace for her when there was no peace,'" declares the Sovereign Lord. (Ezekiel 13:10–16)

Therefore, we must confront large crowds with the narrowness of the road and what it really means to accept Jesus as Lord and Savior. We show them the narrow gate that they must first pass through. In fact, it is so narrow that after many turned away Jesus asked the apostles if they wanted to leave too.

Watch Your Life

I cannot emphasize enough that during this time the crowds watch the lives of those who claim to be Christians. They watch to see if our words match our lives. They watch to see the meaning we give to the words we preach. In other words, our lives give definition to the scriptures we proclaim. Sadly, words can take on a different meaning than what Jesus intended because of the lives of those sharing the gospel. By our lives, we can twist what Jesus really meant. So many proclaim a different gospel by the lack of spirituality in their lives.

As the people saw John's life, they had to admit that their lives lacked something. Likewise, when Joe Sinner sees our lives, he should admit the same. When our lives match the message Jesus brought, then we can speak with the power of the Holy Spirit. I observed this inconsistency between the gospel and the lives of the people in the church where I was baptized. I listened to what they preached, and it was straight from the Bible; however, a conflict began to emerge. They did not define Holy Spirit in the way the Bible did. Their lives did not match up, and this sent me into a tailspin. Be careful that your life matches Jesus' words. Make sure you can say with Paul that your life agrees with what you teach.

> For this reason I am sending to you Timothy, my son whom I love, who is faithful in the Lord. He will remind you of *my way of life* in Christ Jesus, *which agrees* with *what I teach* everywhere in every church. (1 Cor. 4:17, emphasis added)

Hard Teaching

What comes next is the real shocker to Joe Sinner. Just when Joe thinks he has heard and seen almost everything and feels proud that he is getting this doctrinal stuff down, the Holy Spirit finally reveals the seriousness of what it means to give up all for Christ. Then Joe says with so many, "Are only a few going to be saved?"[7] In fact Joe fully agrees with those he heard say, "This is a hard teaching; who can accept it?"[8]

We have become so used to words not meaning anything that at first we just agree with Jesus and try to mimic what He teaches. The Powerful Delusion fools us into thinking we don't really have to obey. Joe Sinner quotes Scripture and talks of humility, and basically has some good doctrine. Yet his own words deceive him because he has not come to despair of self. Being taken in by our own words happens to all who follow Jesus. Unfortunately, most of us remain unwilling to be humbled out of the deception. Joe Sinner has been taken in by his words, and the Word has not yet been formed in him; he only agrees with it.

No man has the new life in him just because he agrees with doctrine. Creating a new life is the work of the cross, and until that happens, the Word is not made complete. Joe finally sees that he has lied to himself. Because he agreed with God on sin, he thought that meant he was dead to it. Joe told God, "Yes, I need to give all to you and to repent." However, at this stage those words come back and hit him across the face like a two-by-four. It is the kindness of God striking him.

> Let a righteous man strike me—it is a kindness; let him rebuke me—it is oil on my head. My head will not refuse it. (Psalm 141:5)

Like the two thieves on the cross, Joe makes a decision for or against the cross. He can be like the first thief who insulted the cross or be like the other who said he deserved the cross in his life.[9] The one who admitted he deserved the cross died on that cross and entered paradise while the other went to hell. Both wanted salvation, but one wanted salvation without the cross. The Powerful Delusion offers this kind of false salvation, promised salvation apart from a crucified life.

When God begins to work the cross in your life, do you tell others that you deserve what God is working?[10] Or do you hope to find someone who will tell you that this cross stuff is not important, that it is a false gospel? Watch yourself carefully at this point because the voices against the cross become loud and united.

The Proper Time

Long before getting to the cross, Joe will probably find many turning around at this point and ceasing to follow Jesus. Joe should let them go. Jesus did not beg them to come back and neither should we. Now Joe might feel in his spirit that Jesus renounces the individuals and towns where he had preached the gospel. They had been taught and shown kindness, yet they refused to repent. Just like Jesus, we may have to renounce "most" of whom we preached the gospel to because they refuse to hate their own lives.

> Then Jesus began to denounce the cities in which most of his miracles had been performed, because they did not repent. (Matthew 11:20)

Now the cost of discipleship, or losing one's life, is declared clearly for all to consider. Here Joe must choose between being a religious traveler with Jesus or becoming a disciple.

As we said before, many turn back when they clearly understand what it will cost them. They go off to find their own churches and preachers who tell them what they want to hear, for many still love self even while doing ministry work. Those who do remain, come close to understanding what the crucified life is all about. The cross gets closer and closer into view, and they willingly surrender just a little more self at each stage.

Indeed Joe Sinner comes mighty close to his first communion with the Lord. Jesus leads him to the table where He can discuss the depth of sinful self and what it really means to be a servant of all. Here Jesus talks about His love, the self that must be crucified, and glorifying God. Sure, He has been talking about this all along, but now Joe really understands the identity of Christ. Here we can begin to talk about some real deep-seated faith that believes "at last!"

> "You believe at last!" Jesus answered. (John 16:31)

174

Followers at this stage will need this belief because the cross will now do its mighty work, and shatter self. Let us really listen to Jesus at this point because, like Joe, we will have to walk the road to Emmaus soon enough—the road of despairing of self and wondering where Jesus is.[11]

Ready for Baptism

They watched Jesus wrestle with sin and discovered they needed to have the same attitude before going to the cross themselves. They counted the cost and listened intently to what Jesus expected, and they still saw it as good news. So few say, "You have the words of eternal life." For the disciples, this teaching was a treasure hidden in a field, and although a man must sell all to have the field, it is no cost to him.[12]

> Simon Peter answered him, "Lord, to whom shall we go? You have the words of eternal life. We believe and know that you are the Holy One of God." (John 6:68–69)

Things usually (though don't hold me to it) move with great speed at this point. Like the rushing wind of Pentecost, the cross, Jesus crucified, and self come sharply and quickly into focus. In other words, Jesus can simply look at us, and it causes us to weep bitterly over our sin. In the past it would have taken a lot of words and many sermons to convince us of sin in our lives. Now all Jesus has to do is look "straight" at us. In days past it would have taken mountains of evidence to convince us of the depth of sin. Now all it takes is the simple crowing of a "rooster." I can always tell how much the cross has been able to do its work in a man's life by how easily he is convicted of sin and how deeply he repents with a "godly sorrow."[13]

We have spiritual maturity when God can just look at us and we know His will and what displeases Him. When it doesn't take a donkey, a light on a road, or a rebuking prophet from God to get through to us, we have become mature in the Lord. If He frowns, we sense and know exactly what to change. If He smiles, we know to rejoice and praise Him. If we do not grow to this point, remember that we put ourselves in danger of being "cursed" and "not acquainted" with righteousness.[14]

> The Lord turned and looked straight at Peter. Then Peter remembered the word the Lord had spoken to him: "Before the rooster crows today, you will disown me three times." And he went outside and wept bitterly. (Luke 22:61–62)

Joe is now tenderhearted and broken, and ready for the Holy Spirit. He is ready for baptism; ready to die to self; ready for God. Joe has counted the cost and willing to hate as Jesus commands and to come after Him. Joe wants to become a disciple and to stop merely traveling with Jesus.

Joe now prepares for water baptism because he feels "cut to the heart" and has understood "many other words" of preaching. Joe again asks, "What shall [I] do?" The hesitation is gone and the religious excuses have disappeared. He simply listens to what God says to "do" is in order to be saved. At this point Joe Sinner becomes Joe Saint.

> "Therefore let all Israel be assured of this: God has made this Jesus, whom you crucified, both Lord and Christ." When the people heard this, they were cut to the heart and said to Peter and the other apostles, *"Brothers, what shall we do?"* Peter replied, "Repent and be baptized, every one of you, in the name of Jesus Christ for the forgiveness of your sins. And you will receive the gift of the Holy Spirit. The promise is for you and your children and for all who are far off—for all whom the Lord our God will call." With many other words he warned them; and he pleaded with them, "Save yourselves from this corrupt generation." Those who accepted his message were baptized, and about three thousand were added to their number that day. (Acts 2:36–41, emphasis added)

If the message is fully[15] preached, everything comes together at water baptism; the love, mercy, blood, cross, and Spirit of Jesus all meet together in agreement. In every case in the Book of Acts, water baptism is the first "do" God has in mind. Of course we are not going to "strain out a gnat and swallow a camel." If someone cannot be water baptized, like the thief on the cross, God will receive him or her. But let no one stand before God guilty of preaching a partial gospel.

We do not have time here for a discussion of water baptism. Rather, let us bring together what part of the gospel we have been looking at: the death to self. For this is exactly what water baptism represents—going into the grave with Jesus and coming out of the tomb with a new life. As the scripture below reveals, those immersed in water enter the tomb with Jesus and come out of the water with a new self. Here the crucifixion to self happens, and we die to sin.

> By no means! We died to sin; how can we live in it any longer? Or don't you know that all of us who were baptized into Christ Jesus were baptized into his death? We were therefore buried with him through baptism into death in order that, just as Christ was raised from the dead through the glory of the Father, we too may live a new life. If we have been united with him like this in his death, we will certainly also be united with him in his resurrection. For we know that our old self was crucified with him so that the body of sin might be done away with, that we should no longer be slaves to sin—because anyone who has died has been freed from sin. (Romans 6:2–7)

The Three Agree

Water baptism is what Peter says "saves" us; however, it does not take away from the blood of Jesus.[16] The Spirit gives life to the water and the blood. For Jesus did not come with just water. He came also with blood and He came by the Spirit.

> . . . sudden flow of blood and water. (John 19:34)

Scripture says that three things are in agreement. When we leave one of those things out of gospel calls, then things really get messed up. 1 John says this is what it means to believe that "Jesus is the Son of God." To believe means to accept that Jesus came with "water," "blood," and "Spirit." We should not leave out water from our gospel calls any more than we would leave out the blood of Jesus. These three agree with each other, and they all give us power to overcome the world.

> Who overcomes the world? Only he who believes that Jesus is the Son of God. This is the one who came by water and blood—Jesus Christ. He did not come by water only, but by water and blood. And the Spirit testifies to this, because the Spirit is Truth. For three testify: the Spirit, the water and the blood; and the three are in agreement. (1 John 5:5–8)

The "blood" is the cost of what it means to follow Jesus. Our life, is in the blood,[17] and it must be poured out unto God so that we might have His blood in us—the blood of His Son.

Although we cannot really separate these three, many churches try to anyway. Some do not like the water, so they leave it out of the message. Others do not like the cost, so they leave out the blood. Still others will not accept the Spirit. Those without the water become legalists and outline-oriented. They enjoy no refreshment or Sabbath rest. Without the water we cannot experience rebirth or new life. Those without the blood become idolaters who like to play in the name of the Lord. Churches with this approach are very entertaining to attend and full of prosperity and happiness. The pastor knows how to joke, preach, and tell story after story, claiming blessings and promising a salvation that will not be delivered. These groups often like to claim the Spirit without the blood. Therefore, self remains alive while they claim the Spirit leads them. These messages have no cost, no sacrifice, no tears, and thus no life in them.

Those who leave out the Spirit are left to their own wisdom as to what is right and wrong in the Lord. They become pure legalists who see themselves as doing God's will. They become their own gods, deciding good from evil. They serve God from their own power and initiative and with rules, guidelines, meetings, fellowship, prayer sessions, and things to do.

Let us ask God to open our hearts and minds to the "full message" of salvation. For only when all three are present, as God intends, is the good news preached.

> "Go, stand in the temple courts," he said, "and tell the people the *full message* of this new life." (Acts 5:20, emphasis added)

As we travel "along the road," sharing with others the "good news about Jesus," let us get around to the cost of having self crucified. Let us share with them the good news of what it means to die to self. Then they will stop the "chariot" and say, "Look, here is water. Why shouldn't I be baptized?"

> Then Philip began with that very passage of scripture and told him the good news about Jesus. As they traveled along the road, they came to some water and the eunuch said, "Look, here is water. Why shouldn't I be baptized?" And he gave orders to stop the chariot. Then both Philip and the eunuch went down into the water and Philip baptized him. When they came up out of the water, the Spirit of the Lord suddenly took Philip away, and the eunuch did not see him again, but went on his way rejoicing. (Acts 8:35–39)

Get "down into the water" with your brother or sister, crucifying and burying the self that must leave his or her life. When you both come "up out of the water," the Spirit of God will send you both on your way rejoicing. Praising God for another brother or sister willing to let God crucify self. Rejoicing that you each have a fellow church member who loves God enough to hate for Jesus.

> "If anyone comes to me and does not hate his father and mother, his wife and children, his brothers and sisters—yes, even his own life—he cannot be my disciple." (Luke 14:26)

This is the beginning of the work of the cross. This is the "obedience that comes from faith" that makes room for God's power to change a man by the way of a crucified life.[18] Any other way to salvation leads to insanity.

Chapter 10

THE CURE

Why do you cry out over your wound, your pain that has no cure? Because of your great guilt and many sins I have done these things to you. (Jeremiah 30:15)

During Jeremiah's lifetime the people cried out because they felt "pain" from their "guilt." They looked far and wide for relief from the "great guilt and many sins," but could not find it. Just like today, people look for restoration in seminars, revival meetings, prayer sessions, sermons, and books, but never find true rest from their guilt. All this activity demonstrates that men and women run from a guilty conscience and they know if they stop to rest, the pains will begin again. We keep on "changing our ways," because to stop and rest before the Lord would expose our sinfulness.[1] Though Jeremiah lived and preached in their midst, they rejected every sermon, every word, and every pleading he proclaimed. Indeed, even after all Jeremiah's predictions came true, the people still refused to repent.[2] So we must also pause and ask ourselves, "Do we really want the cure?"

He has lost connection with the Head, from whom the whole body, supported and held together by its ligaments and sinews, grows as God causes it to grow. (Colossians 2:19)

181

We have "lost connection with the Head" and it shows in our insanity. The cure for insanity in the church comes when we gain again the mind of Christ and fully connect to the "whole body" in spirit, thought, and will. What makes a man sane in Jesus Christ is death to self. Two brains cannot occupy the same space and two minds cannot rule the body. One mind must go. Since our thoughts remain wicked all the time, we must allow Jesus' thoughts to live in us. We must truly be born again in the way and power that Jesus set down, rejecting fully man's religious ways.[3] Self, all that we are, must be put to death by the power of the Holy Spirit.[4] The Powerful Delusion leaves us alive while it claims the blessings of God. This is tantamount to feeding, clothing, and giving shelter to an insane man. Although he may be healthy in body, protected, and fed, he is still mad. As we die to self we "grow" and are "held together" by the power of God. For He always gives a sound mind to those who seek Him with all their heart.

> For God hath not given us the spirit of fear; but of power, and of love, and of a sound mind. (2 Timothy 1:7 KJV)

Only one solution to the insanity can happen in the church today. The answer cannot be found in logic or higher reasoning. After all, what good does it do to teach an insane man lessons in logic? The solution is the cross of Christ and the obedience that comes from it. The cross that crucifies our mind, with its thoughts, feelings, and opinions will give us the mind of Christ.[5] Only the cross connects us back to Jesus so that we can see things as they really are.

It cannot be just any cross, however. It must be the offensive cross of Jesus. The Powerful Delusion has its talk of the cross, but it does not offend the flesh unto death. Whole hosts of individuals give agreement to the need for an offensive cross, but they always disqualify it by saying, "We must not offend." That is equal to telling Jesus that you agree He should die on the cross for sins, but telling him to retire and die peaceably in His bed. A cross that does not offend unto death and whitewashes our deeds will bless them with false humility. There is preaching about the cross, but the hammer and nails that would make that cross a reality in someone's life never happens. The cross the church offends with must not only have hammer and nails, but a whip, thorns, and public humiliation.

When we separate ourselves from the mind of Christ, we become puffed up in "idle notions." The spiritually insane often give complete validation to every thought and emotion. In the church today, "idle notions," passing thoughts and feelings have taken on full credibility. Like madmen, each church has its own feelings and notions that sway it back and forth in madness. And as the Powerful Delusion confirms each madness to be true, the church justifies more insane thoughts. Only the cross can crucify a mind bent on indulging in insanity.

> Do not let anyone who delights in false humility and the worship of angels disqualify you for the prize. Such a person goes into great detail about what he has seen, and his unspiritual mind puffs him up with idle notions. (Colossians 2:18)

Such is the condition in the false church today. The church prays about, glories in, shouts, talks, and writes about in "great detail" every notion that pops up. It reveals an "unspiritual mind," all puffed up with no where to go, like men locked up in a mental institution needing to release useless energy. Only the cross, empowered by the Holy Spirit, can kill such restless flesh.[6] Only the crown of thorns can prick and test dreams, visions, opinions, and idle notions.

Toleration of Sin

The final great insanity we will look at in this book is "Toleration Madness." In the name of toleration, the church allows and supports all manner of sins. Jesus rebuked the church of Thyatira for this sin of toleration. Jesus held "against" them the fact that they "tolerate" certain people.

> "To the angel of the church in Thyatira write: These are the words of the Son of God, whose eyes are like blazing fire and whose feet

are like burnished bronze. I know your deeds, your love and faith, your service and perseverance, and that you are now doing more than you did at first. Nevertheless, I have this against you: You tolerate that woman Jezebel, who calls herself a prophetess. By her teaching she misleads my servants into sexual immorality and the eating of food sacrificed to idols. (Revelation 2:18–20)

Paul rebuked the Corinthian church for their toleration of wickedness. The Corinthian church, like those taken in by the Powerful Delusion, stood "proud" of their acceptance of sin and sinfulness. The amount of wickedness tolerated, justified, and encouraged today in the name of the Lord is appalling. Instead of being "proud" of the toleration everyone should be "filled with grief" at the sin in the church.

It is actually reported that there is sexual immorality among you, and of a kind that does not occur even among pagans: A man has his father's wife. And you are proud! Shouldn't you rather have been filled with grief and have put out of your fellowship the man who did this? (1 Corinthians 5:1–2)

Actually, God's love works in all of this, but it does not manifest itself by tolerating insanity. Jesus blessed the church in Ephesus for their lack of toleration. Jesus knew they could not "tolerate wicked men" and that they even "tested" men who claimed to be something in Jesus. Indeed, they "tested" unto finding "them false." Many gripped by this insanity try to test the hypocrite, but they cannot find anyone "false."

I know your deeds, your hard work and your perseverance. I know that you cannot tolerate wicked men, that you have tested those who claim to be apostles but are not, and have found them false. (Revelation 2:2)

Paul taught the Corinthian church about judging. He declared that with the proper use of spiritual gifts, when everyone is "prophesying" the "unbeliever" will be "judged by all" and convinced that "he is a sinner." He will fall down because "the secrets of his heart will" have been "laid bare." We rarely see this today because God has left and we no longer understand the "testimony" of Jesus.[7] Little wonder that no one falls down in our "worship" services "exclaiming, 'God is really among you!'" We love our sins and remain in love with the toleration insanity sweeping the world.

> But if an unbeliever or someone who does not understand comes in while everybody is prophesying, he will be convinced by all that he is a sinner and will be judged by all, and the secrets of his heart will be laid bare. So he will fall down and worship God, exclaiming, "God is really among you!" (1 Corinthians 14:24–25)

Yes, we must show love to all men, but not toleration of their sin. We need to imitate Jesus, hate the sin *and* the sinner, but lay down our life anyway. The whole notion that we are to hate the sin and love the sinner is a complete lie and a teaching opposed to Jesus Christ. It is a lie about who we are and where we are headed if we do not repent. It makes light of hell and is the soil in which toleration insanity took root. We must love that which we hate, just as God sent His son to love that which He regretted making.[8] And as Christians we are called to love as Jesus loved, to love the unlovable.

The Fear of God

The truth is, as we have seen, we are "worthless" and no good lives in us. Jesus, however, loved the totally corrupted. God loved us, not because of who we are, but because of who He is. He showed unmerited mercy when He died for us and the more we believe and know that, the more we will throw out the toleration gospel. This acceptance of sin robs man of the blessing of knowing how to "fear God." Not many men preach because they "know what it is to fear the Lord." And few have been taught by the cross to "know what it is to fear the Lord" and from that try and "persuade men" to repent. Toleration insanity has no room for that attitude.

Since, then, we know what it is to fear the Lord, we try to persuade men. (2 Corinthians 5:11a)

Friendship With the World

Toleration insanity causes people to forsake the gospel call of Jesus. Instead of preaching repentance, we preach other things in Jesus. Ministries promote tongues, being slain in the Spirit, asking Jesus in your heart, but not true repentance. We give lip service to repentance but people do not walk on the narrow road filled with godly repentance. Instead, the toleration gospel allows man to keep the desires of the flesh, over repentance and death to the flesh. The fruit of this can be seen in both the conservative and charismatic side of the church.

A popular Christian publication reported on the life of a well-known television evangelist. This person was divorced and remarried, and now had a ministry to the gay community. The article repeatedly commended this person for their acceptance and toleration of homosexuals. The evangelist did not openly approve of homosexuality, but allowed them the freedom to be themselves. Throughout the article the tone was one of toleration not one of Jesus' call to repentance. Translation, the salt and light are missing and this person feels no need to repent. Long gone are the words of Jesus.

From that time on Jesus began to preach, "Repent, for the kingdom of heaven is near." (Matthew 4:17)

The misuse of Jesus' statement that we "judge not"[9] in the church bears its fruit.[10] Many easily become upset about the sexual sin of homosexuality in the church, but soon such indignation will disappear. Indeed, adultery, though divorce and remarriage, is no longer viewed as sin. The notion that God's Word declares that couples who remarry are in adultery has almost disappeared from the land.[11] Certainly the wisdom on how to deal with anyone divorced and remarried (in adultery) is gone. Either hard rules are laid down, or toleration and support groups deal with the situation, but rarely will we find the wisdom of the Holy Spirit applied. Now the toleration gospel, something the world has preached for years, receives the seal of approval from even conservative mainline Christians.

Years ago the musicians in the Christian arena began the "crossover" to the world. This crossing over has taken place in every area of the church, and as it happens the world embraces the church. For the world cannot hate the worldly in the church.[12] The insane toleration gospel has taken such a hold of the minds of professing Christians that they do not feel the slightest breath of God's anger preparing to blow. To choose friendship with the world means to become an enemy of God. More and more the church tolerates all manner of sins, impurity, and compromise. Yet no one senses that they became "an enemy of God" by doing so. Indeed, we use the words "no compromise" to promote compromise and it takes a very discerning heart and a strong constitution to stand up against this toleration insanity.

> You adulterous people, don't you know that friendship with the world is hatred toward God? Anyone who chooses to be a friend of the world becomes an enemy of God. (James 4:4)

How few know they are adulterers, deserving of judgment. They have chosen to be friends "of the world" and we must judge them and rebuke them for it. We cannot tolerate their doctrines, lives, works, and projects done in the name of Jesus. Remember, we are to "ignore" those who ignore God's Word about a women's place in church and the order with which worship is conducted.[13] We must, when dead to self, judge them and not even "eat" lunch, dinner, or breakfast with them. We cannot "even eat" with anyone who is "greedy" as the Lord defines greedy, or any "idolater" who does not live a life of "hate."[14]

> But now I am writing you that you must not associate with anyone who calls himself a brother but is sexually immoral or greedy, an idolater or a slanderer, a drunkard or a swindler.

With such a man do not even eat. What business is it of mine to judge those outside the church? Are you not to judge those inside? (1 Corinthians 5:11–12)

Preach Repentance

The disciples did not go out and preach that people are free to be themselves. Hell was too big a reality to the disciples for such mushy toleration gospel calls. They understood all too well the depravity of man and the need for repentance now.[15]

They went out and preached that people should repent. (Mark 6:12)

The message of repentance is so quick and to the point that Jesus declared if people will not repent we must move on. Jesus did not call us to tolerate and let others remain comfortable with who they are. Indeed, Jesus instructed the disciples to give anyone who did not accept the call to repentance a further sign of God's attitude toward them. He said to "shake the dust off" their "feet" as a living, visual rebuke. Jesus calls such action a "testimony against them," a reminder that God will soon judge them.

And if any place will not welcome you or listen to you, shake the dust off your feet when you leave, as a testimony against them." They went out and preached that people should repent. (Mark 6:11–12)

From John the Baptist to Paul, the preaching of Jesus said the love of God manifests itself in calling men to repentance. And if anyone will not accept that repentance, we must shake the dust off our feet and go next door when they oppose us or become abusive.

But when the Jews opposed Paul and became abusive, he shook out his clothes in protest and said to them, "Your blood be on your own heads! I am clear of my responsibility. From now on I will go to the Gentiles." Then Paul left the synagogue and went next door to the house of Titius Justus, a worshiper of God. (Acts 18:6–7)

I have been amazed over the years at how many individuals believe they can disobey Scripture and still escape the insanity in the church. God made it clear, that when a church or Christian does not keep itself pure from the Powerful Delusion, you must separate yourself from them. As we have already seen in 2 Timothy we are to have "nothing" to do with them. Let me repeat it here so that the point might be fully considered.

But mark this: There will be terrible times in the last days. People will be lovers of themselves, lovers of money, boastful, proud, abusive, disobedient to their parents, ungrateful, unholy, without love, unforgiving, slanderous, without self-control, brutal, not lovers of the good, treacherous, rash, conceited, lovers of pleasure rather than lovers of God—having a form of godliness but denying its power. Have nothing to do with them. (2 Timothy 3:1–5)

In the Scripture below, Peter warns us not to allow their "empty words to deceive us." "Empty words" that seek to "deceive" us into believing such people go to heaven. Often individuals will ask, "Can a person be saved in such compromising churches?" God can even use Balaam's donkey to speak His will, but if they are saved it will be in spite of, not through those churches. God blessed Israel through Balaam, but not because of anything good about Balaam.[16] The Holy Spirit will lead anyone to leave such churches and false Christians. "For of this you can be sure . . ."

No immoral, impure or greedy person—such a man is an idolater—has any inheritance in the kingdom of Christ and of God. Let no one deceive you with empty words, for because of such things God's wrath comes on those who are disobedient. Therefore do not be partners with them. (Ephesians 5:5–7)

What we have described in this book makes it clear that such individuals, without fully repenting, do not have "any inheritance" in Jesus. Do not "deceive" yourself by saying that God has not called you to leave such churches and Christians; He just called you. As Ephesians stated, they are "impure" and that word certainly describes the insanity in the church. A madman has moments of sanity, but soon slips back into foolishness. If you desire God, above men and all things, then only obedience will protect you. You simply cannot be "partners with them" and enter heaven. By associating with these individuals you tell God that you love their approval and sins more than Him and His holiness. So why should He accept you into heaven? After all Jesus didn't come to earth to die for unrepentant sinners, He came to save those who love God more than their own lives. Unselfish lovers of God is what God desires.[17]

> They overcame him by the blood of the Lamb and by the word of their testimony; they did not love their lives so much as to shrink from death. (Revelation 12:11)

If we want a sane mind, a sure salvation in Jesus then let us not shrink from death to our thoughts and ways. If we do not run from the Holy Spirit who seeks to put us on the cross, God will spare us from believing "the lie." If we do not fear death to self as we carry our daily cross, we will not fail in that hour when the anti-Christ demands our lives.[18] We will overcome the Powerful Delusion, by the power of the Lamb. For the power of the Lamb is found in the blood He shed on the cross and as we pour out our life His life will flow into us.

As we walk led by the spirit, we go the way of Jesus, step by step. Each step costs a man more of his life, of his part in this world. As it was with Jesus, it will be with us, otherwise we are not of Him. "In this way, love is made complete among us so that we will have confidence on the day of judgement, because in this world we are like him," 1 John 4:17 promises. If we are not like Him in this world we should have no "confidence" of salvation awaiting us on "judgement" day.

Lawlessness

It all comes down to love, love for God, and then love expressed for our fellow man—not a love defined by our opinions, nor by the Powerful Delusion, but what God calls love. Think of the Powerful Delusion, it is at the root of disobedience. Everything in this book comes down to one simple issue, will we be obedient or disobedient. The anti-Christ is a "man of lawlessness" and his spirit teaches us how to disobey God. Satan attempts with great effort to work a spirit of lawlessness in the church while declaring we have salvation. As Satan told Eve, "You will not surely die." To state that this deception works is a major understatement. As the Scripture below shows us, before the anti-Christ can come on the scene, a "rebellion" must occur. That rebellion happens in the church as well as in the world. This book has exposed only a small fraction of the rebellion against God's Word occuring in the church. If repentance cannot be seen on these few easy to understand issues, what hope is there for the average church goer? Don't be decieve[d]" about the rebellion sweeping the church.

> Don't let anyone deceive you in any way, for that day will not come until the rebellion occurs and the man of lawlessness is revealed, the man doomed to destruction. (2 Thessalonians 2:3)

It is a "secret power of lawlessness." This lawlessness enters into people's lives by stealth. They don't know it is happening to them. It slips in so slyly while they read their Bibles. It enters in as they fold hands to pray, lift voices to praise, and come forward to be saved. It is a power that manifests itself with all that we have looked at and more. Soon God will not "hold[s]" back the influence and like a great flood it will sweep the world.

> For the secret power of lawlessness is already at work; but the one who now holds it back will continue to do so till he is taken out of the way. (2 Thessalonians 2:7)

Millions sit in pews, unable to detect this influence because it is a "secret power," yet its fruit is easy to see. Either we will obey what we have examined or be lawless in our approach to God. It all depends on where you stand. If you side with those who are "free in Christ" to refuse obedience to Scripture, then your answered prayers are the work of the Powerful Delusion. If you stand with those who are "free in Christ" from their sinful nature so that you can obey Scripture, there is hope of salvation.[19]

The anti-Christ will ask for faith, a belief in himself, that will come out in disobedience to God. Those who have an honest saving belief in Jesus will be known by their obedience. This is how you can know who loves God and who truly loves his fellow man. If a man states that he loves me, but refuses to obey what we have looked at here (and more), he is a liar. Scripture is clear, "This is how we know that we love the children of God: by loving God and carrying out his commands." The spirit of lawlessness defines belief in Jesus differently than God. Believing on the Lord Jesus according to God is the same as obedience.[20] Notice in the Scripture below how belief and obedience weave together to make one complete garment of salvation. The lawless one seeks to rip that garment from the seams.

> Everyone who believes that Jesus is the Christ is born of God, and everyone who loves the father loves his child as well. This is how we know that we love the children of God: by loving God and carrying out his commands. This is love for God: to obey his commands. And his commands are not burdensome, for everyone born of God overcomes the world. This is the victory that has overcome the world, even our faith. Who is it that overcomes the world? Only he who believes that Jesus is the Son of God. (1 John 5:1–5)

Those infected with the insanity of the Powerful Delusion find God's commands "burdensome," legalistic, and a salvation by works issue. We "overcome" the world and the lawlessness of the Powerful Delusion by our obedience. An obedience that is by faith.

> Through him and for his name's sake, we received grace and apostleship to call people from among all the Gentiles to the *obedience that comes from faith.* (Romans 1:5)

The Powerful Delusion at first slowly began to delude the church, but with each passing year it pushes forward with ever increasing speed. Satan has taken each church and ministry's disobedience to specific Scriptures and used that for a foothold to work ever increasing lawlessness. What was written off as matters of opinion or differences of doctrine, became a beachhead for Satan to land upon. After all, it is total sin to *agree to disagree.* We are all called to perfect unity and only a refusal to surrender self keeps the church from this unity. The church rejected the cross that could work complete unity because men did not want to give up their sin and refused the power of the cross.[21] All of this has deluded the church and those taken in by the power of the delusion will have no grace to resist the "mark" of the beast. In fact, they will "worship the beast."

How can a person know if they will take the mark? By their level of obedience to God's commands in the Holy Spirit. For it is either lawlessness or obedience. An obedience to God that comes through "endurance" and "faithful[ness] to Jesus." Obedience provides the cure for the insanity that blinds a man by the Powerful Delusion. In short, the cross.

Will it be for you a "smoke of" "torment" that "rises for ever and ever" or a "saint who obey[ed] God's commandments?" A "faithfulness" to Jesus that can be seen in Holy Spirit inspired obedience.

> And the smoke of their torment rises for ever and ever. There is no rest day or night for those who worship the beast and his image, or for anyone who receives the mark of his name. This calls for patient endurance on the part of the saints who obey God's commandments and remain faithful to Jesus. (Revelation 14:11–12)

EVERYTHING SAID

With all of this said, look to the offensive message of the cross that has the power to save you from the Powerful Delusion.

For the message of the cross is foolishness to those who are perishing, but to us who are being saved it is the power of God. (1 Corinthians 1:18)

ENDNOTES

Chapter 1—The Lie

1. John 12:25
2. An understanding of the time period in which we live and how to see through false miracles is detailed in my book, A Whisper Revival—Our Only Option (WinePress Publishing).
3. 1 Peter 4:1
4. James 1:22
5. Luke 23:31
6. Mark 8:35

Chapter 2—Insanity

1. Mark 10:18
2. 2 Corinthians 12:11

Chapter 3—Numbers Madness

1. Romans 8:17
2. Mark 13:19
3. Philippians 2:12
4. Acts 4:13
5. John 3:27
6. 1 Corinthians 2:4
7. 1 Corinthians 2:5
8. 1 Corinthians 2:2
9. Luke 2:35

Chapter 4—Great Things Madness

1. Luke 7:47
2. Galatians 2:20
3. Jeremiah 23:21–22
4. John 12:24
5. Galatians 6:17
6. The common belief based on Scriptures from Romans, taken out of context, that turns salvation into simple, easy steps of just accepting, believing, and confessing.
7. 1 John 2:6
8. Luke 3:7
9. Luke 17:10
10. 1 Samuel 21:14–15
11. Luke 22:44
12. Luke 22:42
13. John 6:65
14. 2 Corinthians 8:9
15. Acts 20:35
16. 2 Timothy 4:3
17. 2 Corinthians 13:11
18. Even The Demons Believe
19. Mark 8:35
20. 2 Corinthians 10:18
21. Matthew 11:30
22. Psalm 106:25
23. Hebrews 11:35
24. Matthew 5:5, new heaven

Chapter 5—Authority Madness

1. Romans 8:17, Luke 8:13, Hebrews 11:38, Philippians 2:6–8
2. John 8:28
3. Philippians 2:3
4. Titus 2:5
5. Titus 2:3–5
6. Colossians 3:11
7. Isaiah 40:26
8. Judge 17:6
9. Romans 8:19
10. Matthew 25:33
11. Hebrews 8:5
12. Luke 12:7
13. Colossians 3:17
14. 1 Timothy 1:19

Chapter 6—Money Madness

1. 2 Corinthians 8:9
2. Mark 10:21
3. 1 Timothy 6:8
4. Matthew 6:25
5. Luke 14:26
6. 1 Corinthians 1:17
7. Ecclesiastes 11:8
8. 1 Timothy 5:18
9. Psalms 132:1
10. 2 Corinthians 6:10
11. Galatians 4:13
12. Malachi 3:18

Chapter 7—Miracle Madness

1. 1 Peter 4:1
2. Luke 23:31
3. 2 Corinthians 12:4
4. 2 Corinthians 12:7
5. Ecclesiastes 7:2, Matthew 5:4
6. Luke 14:26
7. John 12:24
8. Mark 1:23
9. 2 Corinthians 3:3
10. 1 Corinthians 2:11, John 6:63
11. Ecclesiastes 5:1–2

Chapter 8—Pleasure Madness

1. Luke 9:14
2. John 4:32
3. Mark 6:39
4. Mark 8:6
5. Acts 18:27
6. Acts 16:14
7. Luke 11:25
8. Matthew 23:15
9. 1 Corinthians 6:13
10. Hebrews 11:25, 1 John 2:15
11. Revelation 21:7
12. 1 Corinthians 10:5
13. James 4:4

Chapter 9—Altar Call Madness

1. Even The Demons Believe, by Timothy Williams
2. Luke 19:4
3. John 6:44
4. John 4:39
5. Luke 3:16
6. 1 Chronicles 21:1
7. Luke 13:23
8. John 6:60
9. Luke 23:41
10. Mark 15:31
11. Luke 24:13
12. Matthew 13:44
13. 2 Corinthians 7:10–11
14. Hebrews 5:1–6:8
15. Acts 5:20
16. 1 Peter 3:21
17. Leviticus 17:11
18. Romans 1:5

Chapter 10—The Cure

1. Jeremiah 2:36
2. Jeremiah 44:15–18
3. Romans 10:3
4. Romans 8:13
5. 1 Corinthians 2:16
6. Psalm 131:2
7. Revelation 19:10
8. Genesis 6:6
9. Luke 6:37
10. If the cross were understood, then individuals would understand that Jesus meant that *we* are not to judge, but that does not exclude Jesus judging through us. This is how Peter knew the "heart" of Ananias (Acts 5:3), he was dead to his own judgments and had the mind of Christ. Therefore it was not Peter who judged, but Jesus in him who did the judging. There is not time to discuss this doctrine here, but if one will take this concept to the book of John, it will be easy to see in the life of Jesus.
11. Scripture is clear that a married couple is bound in a marriage until one of the partners dies. "A woman is bound to her husband as long as he lives. But if her husband dies, she is free to marry anyone she wishes, but he must belong to the Lord." (1 Corinthians 7:39) When Paul speaks of not being "bound" in a circumstance He means that if a partner will not live in peace with a Christian, the believer is not to try and keep the marriage together. They must let the unbeliever go, to "let him do so." (1 Corinthians 7:15). They may divorce, but they cannot remarry until death has occurred (1 Corinthians 7:11). As Scripture states when a divorce does occur, ". . . she must remain unmarried or else be reconciled to her husband. And a husband must not divorce his wife." The reason for this is that no one knows if a husband or wife will come to the Lord later on and the marriage restored. "How do you know, wife, whether you will save your husband? Or, how do you know, husband,

whether you will save your wife?" (1 Corinthians 7:16). When Jesus stated that one cannot divorce except for adultery He addressed the issue of adultery, not remarriage. In other words, if someone commits adultery and they are divorced, the person divorcing them is not causing them to commit adultery. But if someone divorces for any other reason than adultery, they force the other person into a position of remarriage and therefore adultery, (see Matthew 5:32). If someone divorces because the partner committed adultery, they don't cause that person to commit adultery because the sin had already been committed. Jesus was quite clear, anyone who marries a divorced person commits adultery. "Anyone who divorces his wife and marries another woman commits adultery, and the man who marries a divorced woman commits adultery." (Luke 16:18) If you find yourself in a position of being divorced and remarried don't just assume you are to separate, guidance from the Holy Spirit from a crucified life will be needed. Of course don't assume you are to stay together either.

12. John 15:18
13. 1 Corinthians 14:38
14. Luke 14:25–27
15. Luke 3:9
16. Deuteronomy 23:5
17. John 18:9
18. Romans 8:13
19. Luke 1:74
20. James 2:14
21. Philippians 3:15, 1 Corinthians 1:10, Acts 4:32

To order additional copies of

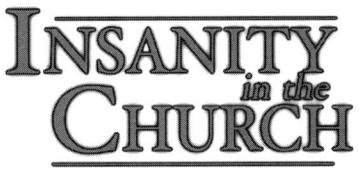

Have your credit card ready and call

Toll free: (877) 421-READ (7323)

or send $12.95* each plus $4.95 S&H** to

WinePress Publishing
PO Box 428
Enumclaw, WA 98022

www.winepresspub.com

*WA residents, add 8.4% sales tax

**add $1.00 S&H for each additional book ordered

Other books written by Timothy Williams:

Even the Demons Believe
- This book examines how Jesus made Christians while contrasting it with today's salvation calls. This book is a great tool for introducing non-believers to Christ, as well as giving Christians a fresh look at their salvation.
- ISBN 1-57921-355-3

The Essential Piece
- This book examines why Jesus said *anyone* who follows Him *must* hate his own life.
- ISBN 1-57921-293-x

A Whisper Revival
- This book explains how God wants to lead us to the "quiet waters" (Psalm 23:2) where we can honestly be revived.
- ISBN 1-57921-274-3

101 Ways to Deny Self
- This book gives 101 practical ways in which to live out Jesus' command in Luke 9:23: *Then he said to them all: "If anyone would come after me, he must deny himself . . ."*
- ISBN 1-57921-397-9

Also, by Timothy Williams' helpmate:

As You Walk Along the Way, by Carla Williams
- This book explains how you can lead your child on the path of spiritual discipline.
- ISBN 0-88965-187-6

Sound Doctrine
PO Box 856
Enumclaw, WA 98022

Phone: (360) 802-2550

Notes

Notes

Notes

Notes

Notes